AF325812

In the Lion's Den

Married to a Narcissistic Pervert

Marianne Guillemin

IN THE LION'S DEN

Married to a Narcissistic Pervert

Max Milo
TÉMOIGNAGE

Max Milo Éditions
Paris, 2023
www.maxmilo.com
ISBN : 978-2-315-01223-7

To my children whom I love so much...

PROLOGUE

This story is inspired by a true story. My story.

The ten years I spent living alongside a perverted personality could have destroyed me, and left a strong imprint on the woman I've become. It took me time, a lot of time, and help to be able to look back on this period of my life without shame or (too much) guilt. Today I understand better, I accept my share of responsibility and, above all, I'm convinced that I acted in the best possible way. There was nothing else to do. Escape, distance myself and put the pieces of my life back together.

I think most women stay in these terrible situations because they don't want to admit they've made a mistake. For years I told myself that things would work out, that he wasn't just this violent, temperamental man because I had loved him, it was inconceivable that I could have felt love for someone who was destroying me.

I'd had a happy, sheltered childhood, raised by a loving grandmother after my father's death, then by my mother and a lovely stepfather. I was the eldest of five siblings, three brothers and a sister with whom I got on well. I was the first to marry.

I knew what love was, I had seen a couple who loved each other, my mother had taught me the joy of living, I don't even have the excuse of a sad life that would have thrown me into the arms of the first man I met. I'd been taught to trust, to respect each other, to feel secure in shared feelings.

What happened? I'd made a mistake about the person, and this initial error buried my head and heart in the sand. I preferred to forget the difficult moments and concentrate on the positive. Because life with a pervert isn't woven into the spinning wheel of misfortune. No, the threads cross, alternating between joyful moments, tenderness, shared projects and desires that made me believe that happiness was possible, within reach and with good will.

Then, when my eyes finally opened, when I took stock of the difficult moments and the rare happy ones, I wanted to help him change. I understood the pathological nature of his character, his chronic inability to be happy, his constant search for drama. I tried to understand him, to pinpoint what it was in his childhood experience that had led to this deviance. A mother who was hard but nonetheless fused, a father who was absent and failing, and above all, a sexual assault in adolescence that no one really took into account. He was sent to a boarding school in Switzerland on the orders of his godfather, a doctor who must have understood the urgency of the situation (after all, he had spent six months on his bed, refusing to go to school!) But no words of comfort were ever spoken to him.

I naively thought that with love I could change him. But perverts have no access to love. They seek immediate pleasure, their personal pleasure even in their suffering, from which they derive a certain pleasure. So I tried to change myself, to be a person more suited to his character. I avoided upsetting him, I spoke as little as possible, in short I became a shadow with a single objective: to avoid conflict.

Faced with the evidence, I finally admitted that my husband had something to do with a mental disorder. I managed to get him to see a psychiatrist, who confirmed the diagnosis but didn't specify what it was. Various treatments were tried, including mood regulators, and there was a slight improvement. But the acceptance of his illness was not a smooth process, and soon he was refusing treatment.

He wasn't ill, he said, he just had behavioral problems. He sometimes admitted it, but stressed that these problems were a function of the people around him (i.e. me). And it's true that I was catalyzing his anger, increasing his irritation if I trembled when he raised his voice. It was a vicious circle.

I realized then that I'd come full circle. I tried to change him with love, then I tried to change myself, out of love; then I asked the medical profession for help and one day, I'm not sure when, the love disappeared.

But I didn't leave immediately. Duty and pride replaced feelings. I was still looking for solutions, but I began to protect myself and above all my children. I set up avoidance strategies; I was lucky enough to have a busy job and friends: I drew strength from these moments spent away from home to face it with detachment.

If it hadn't been for the violence and constant nervous tension, I'd have stayed even longer. I imagined that it was better for the children, that their living conditions were better this way (whereas this period damaged them, on the contrary) and above all, deep down, I was afraid. Fear of not being able to get out of it, fear of not being able to escape him and fearing reprisals, helpless, not knowing where to go and above all where to start to put my life in order.

No one had forced me to marry him, and some of my friends had even tried to dissuade me. Or, at least, tried to make me think again. I was young, I had time. "Why did you get married?" someone asked one day. "Because he asked me to." It's as simple, as stupid as that answer. And as I thought about it, I realized that I'd gotten myself into this mess...

At this stage, I had moments of intense discouragement when the idea of disappearing would cross my mind. Where the idea of suppressing him, of pushing him out of the window when he leaned over the railing shouting that he was going to jump, in his delirious fits, would surprise and shame me afterwards.

I owe my children the courage to leave and take charge of my life.

After trying everything to give them a family with a normal father, I finally understood and admitted that I had failed. That the life I was making them endure between their father and me was hell, and that my duty was no longer to save my marriage but to protect my children.

It was the only thing to do and I delayed too long, trapped as I was in the clutches of a tyrant I'd thought I loved.

Today, I'm able to dismantle the mechanism of this relationship and understand its inner workings. What helped me was that I never saw myself as a victim. I claim my share of responsibility and I believe that to get out of it, you have to be willing to take charge of your life and therefore accept your faults, so as to be able to bounce back. Wanting to regain control, even when you feel lost: if you really want to get out of this, you're well on your way. Don't suffer, don't remain in the role of victim.

Even at the bottom of the abyss, when all self-esteem is shattered, when others make you believe you're incapable, keep intact the little light that makes you believe in yourself.

Lurking in humility and fear, the better to jump up and fly away when the time comes. Admit to yourself that you're unhappy, that this isn't the life you'd dreamed of. To stop telling yourself that everything's fine, that everything's going to work out, when in fact things are getting worse.

But once again, thanks to my work and my friends, I've been able to break out of my isolation and keep a little lucidity alive. I've hoarded it like a treasure, to be used when the time comes.

I have no regrets, this difficult time led me to lasting happiness, my children have become wonderful adults and today I can say, more than twenty years later: I've made it.

I've known women who have lived through things as terrible, if not worse, than mine. Women who had fewer cards in their hand, because they had no job, no family, because they were foreigners. And I've seen a number of them, like me, driven by the strength to offer their children another life. I met them and their lives resembled mine; the wolf was there, taking up all the space.

It's possible to get out of it, I know that today, and only today am I able to talk about it.

May my story enlighten the women who are still suffering, and give them the strength to overcome their tyrants.

Chapter 1

I was 20, he was 31.

I was flattered, no doubt, reassured because what he was proposing was similar to what I knew. Marriage, a family, children.

I was finishing my journalism studies and was doing a TV internship.

That's where I met him.

My head was full of plans, but I was afraid of everything, especially life. I wanted to be free, yet I needed to love. I'd thought I was in love several times before, but life had quickly swept aside those youthful stories. I didn't think anyone would want me. Yet I was cheerful, dynamic, pretty in the end, at least enough to please, even if most of the time I frightened men away with my excessive vitality. I wanted everything, right away.

He was a journalist and I admired him. He had succeeded where I was just starting out, and I was flattered by his sound advice. He took the trouble to correct me, to explain things to me, the little intern at the *desk*, and his interest went straight to my heart.

When he invited me to the cinema the first time, he seemed delighted to see that we shared the same tastes (Woody Allen,

English cinema, etc.). I found that, for a man, he had a rare sensitivity, he felt things intuitively, and we could talk for hours over a film.

We shared a taste for talking: dissecting, debating, analyzing. I was proud to be considered a worthy interlocutor, because he seemed so cultured and erudite. And when he cut me off or silenced me, far from seeing it as a sign of tyranny or authoritarianism, I thought he was probably right and that I was too young to know. So I listened to him religiously, happy for him to take me to dinner, and then to take me home.

He had an apartment in a nice neighborhood, above his parents' house. I should have known better. After all, he was over 30... The first night I stayed with him, he told me not to make any noise and to get up slowly so that his mother wouldn't hear that he wasn't alone in the apartment... Every day, she went upstairs to make her son's bed and put the evening meal on a little tray. I found this touching: I'd barely outgrown childhood myself and, later on, I found it very practical to have this spare mother at home, or nearly so.

He said I lifted his spirits, that I was alive; that was his expression: "You're so alive." I felt I existed for someone for the first time.

Soon after we met, he started calling me every day, taking me out to the country at weekends. We went to exhibitions and restaurants. I thought our story was off to a good start, even if, at the time, my main concern was finishing my studies and finding a job.

In the summer I left for my end-of-year internship at *Le Dauphiné Libéré* in Grenoble. I was happy, I liked the job.

I lived in an apartment lent to me by one of my uncles, right in the center of town. He would come and join me every weekend, and send me lovely letters the rest of the time. He said he couldn't live without me. Summers were warm and bright, and on Sundays we went hiking in the mountains.

In September, my editor-in-chief asked me to stay on. I wanted to accept; I was blossoming in my work, and the region was very beautiful. I hardly hesitated. But he begged me to come back to Paris. He talked to me for hours on the phone to convince me, and of course I loved this persistence, I took it as a sign of attachment. I now know that he simply couldn't stand anything or anyone slipping through his fingers. If I'd come back in September without saying a word, would he have been so eager? I understood much later that I always had to make him believe that I'd given in, that he'd won, or else he'd lose interest immediately, or even feel a contradiction in his desires that would make him explode.

He had no trouble showing me that I still had a year's study ahead of me to write a dissertation, and that it was a pity to do it by correspondence, without putting all the chances on my side. Besides, he told me, he had connections and would help me with my internships...

Sometimes I think my life would have been so different if I'd stayed there. We would have lost touch, I would have become a columnist, I would have married a mountain man...

Especially as I should have been more receptive: I'd already caught a glimpse of his character.

We'd gone for a bike ride one Sunday when he'd come to join me. On the way back, I was tired and put my foot down on an uphill slope. IIe turned around and started shouting at me:

"Are you coming back up? I'm not waiting for you!

- Don't wait up for me, I've got a stitch in my side, see you at home...

Furious, he got off his bike and came up to me:

- But you can make an effort, if you can't keep up with me there's no point in cycling together!"

I was pissed off, tired, and gave him a sharp reply. He left; when I got home, he was packing his suitcase. I thought it was ridiculous to argue just because I didn't have the same stamina as him. I tried to explain it to him calmly, but he was furious. When I came out of the shower, he was there, smiling, preparing dinner and serving me a drink. I was relieved he'd stayed and threw myself into his arms, apologizing: "What a baby you are..." he said, stroking my hair...

The trap was in place. He'd already figured out how to manipulate me. The wolf had just slipped his mask a little, so little... But I'd caught sight of him, quickly, he'd surprised me, but I wasn't scared yet. I hadn't quite understood his change of heart and immediately thought it was a misunderstanding.

The wolf, that day, returned to his den... The rest of the evening passed pleasantly, and I put out of my mind this ridiculous scene, which I attributed to mutual fatigue...

But deep down, it was perhaps these initial hiccups that drew me to the idea of staying in Grenoble, waiting a while before joining him in Paris. At the same time, part of me agreed with him that I had to finish my dissertation. He loved me and offered to let me live with him. Wasn't it wonderful, this life to build for me instead of working alone in this unknown city doing local news?

So I came back to enroll in my third year and moved in with him. More out of convenience than true love, because what he was offering me, this life for two, resembled what I knew, a certain normality.

I was doing freelance work in newspapers and on the radio. Nothing very secure, but he really pushed me to finish my studies.

Strangely enough, he always pushed me to work, to study, as if he wanted to be proud of me, and at the same time I never did enough and he was always criticizing me. It was a constant paradox that he was able to support me to the hilt to get a job or an interview, and then reproach me endlessly, insisting that it was all thanks to him, as if he was feeding off a permanent gratitude he could never get enough of. I never failed to praise his interventions, to report the slightest word of praise about him, to make sure I never put myself forward, lest he should, with a curt word, belittle and immediately minimize my action. He wanted to be in control, because I was his thing, and my failures would hit him with anger, while my successes were rightfully his.

He wanted us to get married and the future suddenly seemed enchanting. What better proof of love could there be for the simpleton I was at the time? He wanted to link his life to mine, it was a fairy tale, I was barely out of school, he was a great reporter and he'd chosen me!

Was I blinded by his much-needed attention? For other details should already have alerted me. I'd had trouble fitting my few little student things into his apartment. He had me throw out my stuffed animals, my bric-a-brac as he called it, tolerating my desk and dressing table in a corner, my books in boxes (it must have taken me years to get them onto shelves) and my clothes in the hall closet. Listen," he'd argued, "you can see that this apartment has style, cachet, you're not going to disorganize everything..."

It's true that his place was pretty: well-waxed antique furniture, brand-new carpeting, a fully-equipped kitchen... I told myself that he was probably right, that he had good taste and that, little by little, I'd make the place my own.

But it was never possible. I could never hang a picture or move a piece of furniture without his permission, which he rarely gave.

I had entered his life, but I had no say in it. I was part of the scenery. I was young, I told myself it was normal, that this was his home and I had to adapt. Under his guidance, I learned to clean, dust and tidy. He was a maniac, and I didn't want to upset him over what I called details. My things had to be put away all the time (like the children's later on) and not show up. A visiting friend once told me, years later: "I'd never have imagined that three children lived here, there's nothing, not a toy, not a coat...".

And I, stupidly, took this remark as a compliment. The bed was squared away, the vacuum cleaned every morning before leaving, the dishes washed, wiped and tidied, a veritable model apartment. I wanted to please him, order was second nature to him and I brushed aside this constraint, thinking that if it was enough to satisfy him, it would have been foolish of me not to play along...

Especially as I wasn't really into tidying up when I was 20. Today, however, I fold and put away the day's clothes and avoid leaving things lying around, even when I'm alone. The imprint is still there, too strong. But I can tell myself that I've turned it into a quality. I'd rather tidy up after my own people than observe their compulsive tendency to put everything in order...

At first, I'd sometimes tell him that complaining about glasses not being wiped up seemed a bit disproportionate; I'd try to get him thinking about something else, and bring up his work, a subject he loved because it made him feel valued. I still managed to cheer him up, and his bad moods never lasted.

Was he making an effort? Was he less shady? Above all, I think he was so cunning and manipulative that he understood at the beginning of our relationship that I could still back out. That if I was unhappy, if his temper frightened me, it wouldn't be long before I left him.

His claws hadn't yet closed in on my life, and he could feel it.

His efforts were always calculated. He was therefore capable of making efforts, even transforming himself, not to achieve happiness or to make me happy, but only to reach his goal. Once I'd achieved my goal, the mask would fall off quite quickly, and I'd rarely see the face of the man who'd seduced me.

The pervert needs an object, or to be more precise, a person whom he reduces to the status of an object. And to achieve this, he simulates love and kindness by any means necessary. And contrary to what I used to think - he shrouded his actions in a kind of sickly unconsciousness - everything is premeditated. He's driven by impulse, of course, but his actions are channeled into satisfying his angers; they don't lead him into impulsiveness, and that's why he has no remorse or regret, even when he pretends to feel it.

He pushed me to work, directed me towards newspapers, but systematically denigrated all my projects. I worked hard, even though I didn't earn much. In fact, he helped me, coming up with ideas, correcting my articles and referring me to colleagues. He criticized my work a lot, but his remarks were often well-founded, he was experienced and I thought it was nice of him to take an interest in what I was doing.

I wanted to live up to his expectations, but it took me a while to realize that the bar was always going to be higher...

I introduced him to my parents. He was kind, intelligent, well-mannered and had a situation: my parents found him perfect.

For his part, his family were relieved, as his mother feared (and rightly so) that he would never marry... If I'd been smarter and had already put together the few pieces of the puzzle that were lying around, I would have dug deeper... He had an older sister with whom he maintained a distant relationship, made up of arguments against a backdrop of latent jealousy. He was the favorite, the cherished son; his sister was a negligible quantity. Later on, my mother-in-law made a real distinction between our children, whom she adored, and her daughter's, whom she saw little of and criticized all the time.

We were married in Brittany, at my parents' home, in April 1980. Less than a year after we met.

I thought I was in love. In fact, he had chosen me and I was happy, flattered, relieved. I knew he had a difficult character, but I also knew that he wasn't as happy or self-confident as he let on. I felt invested with a mission: to give him happiness, joie de vivre. I knew how to do it, I had a happy personality and I'd been brought up to be affectionate and secure.

I told myself that he would change, that he would blossom, that he would be fine and then all his little foibles would fade away.

I hadn't realized that he was simply unfit for happiness.

The day before our wedding, we left Paris for Brittany.

He had just bought a motorhome. It was our first project, going on vacation as the roads dictated. We were going to the Alps on our honeymoon. I'd have to say it was his plan, not mine; I'd gone along with it to please him, but I wasn't comfortable in cramped interiors, and the prospect of wild camping didn't thrill me...

We took turns driving, even though I'd only just got my license. It was he who had taught me to drive his Fiat 127, and when I returned triumphant from the test, he took out a bottle of champagne and exclaimed: "You can thank me, let's drink to your excellent instructor, yet you gave me such a hard time!"

I wasn't even shocked by this approach; I think I was already conditioned.

After that, he admitted he didn't like driving and let me take the wheel most of the time, but that didn't stop him deafening me with criticism.

That day, as I was driving our motorhome to Brittany, he ended up swearing at me, shouting so much that I pulled over to the side of the road and got out, telling him to take the wheel. He shifted on the seat, slammed the door and sped off. I stood stunned in the pouring rain, not knowing what to do. I was walking ahead when I saw the truck stopped a little further on.

He opened the door: "Get in!" he said, "and stop behaving like a child, if I make remarks it's for your own good, you don't know how to drive!"

I cried and said no more until we arrived at my parents' house.

There he was charming, relaxed and pleasant. My mother thought I looked pale.

I could see my mother-in-law, my brothers and my sister coming, as if in a fog.

Could I have stopped it all with a single word? I was afraid of making a mistake, of missing something important, of losing him. I already felt guilty.

On April 7 1980, I said "I do" in the church of Dirinon, for better or for worse.

Without knowing that the worst was indeed yet to come.

I was already in the jaws of my chosen wolf.

I was about to turn 21.

CHAPTER 2

For our honeymoon, he wanted to go skiing. He loved the mountains, I preferred the sea. I told him I was a terrible skier, but he didn't seem to mind. I suggested a little trip abroad, but he replied: "Listen, spending so much money to go to the end of the world, I don't see the point…".

I'd felt ridiculous, with cheesy desires, so I'd nodded quickly when he'd mentioned the Alps.

His desires, opinions and tastes always seemed more legitimate than mine. He'd dismiss my arguments with a wave of his hand, arguing that my youth and inexperience gave me no say in the matter. And he was so sure of himself, and suddenly sometimes so aggressive, that his opinion imposed itself like a thunderstorm rumbling in the distance of everyday life. And before long, the nervous tension that filled the room when we disagreed took my breath away. I ended up with a single goal: to find peace again, to keep the storm at bay, to do everything I could to ease the tension. When I had dared to mention the idea of a trip to the sun, I had immediately sensed that the conflict was simmering, swelling like a wave. I'd quickly added that I'd be delighted to discover the mountains with him, and the wave had collapsed on the sand of our discussion. He was smiling again and I was calm.

We arrived in Les Arcs, the studio was nice and, the very next day, my brand-new husband was training me on a black run. On the chairlift, I reminded him that I was just a beginner... He laughed and, once at the top, grabbed his poles and disappeared.

I was panicked.

Finally, I took my courage and my poles in both hands, and from slalom to snowplough, I managed to glide as best I could on this cursed track.

It took me an hour and a half to get back down. I met him again at the end of the morning, delighted. When he saw me arriving on my snowplough at the edge of the blue run, he burst out laughing: "But it's true that you don't know how to ski! How is that possible?"

He soon left me alone and, to tell the truth, I was rather relieved. I was getting to know him and I feared he might repeat the episode on the black trail...

He didn't even notice that by the end of the second day, I'd stopped buying my pass. Instead, I went for some nice walks. It was the off-season, so there weren't too many people around, and I really learned to appreciate the wilderness, walking in untouched snow. Deep down, I already preferred to be alone, and he was having so much fun on his skis, he didn't need me and left me in peace. We only saw each other at dinners, which were punctuated by stories of his exploits. He'd clean his gear and check the weather. I found him fit and relaxed, and had already learned to match my mood to his, making the most of these moments of relaxation. Eight days after our wedding, I was already used to being better off without him...

"What about skiing?" asked my father-in-law, to whom I had confided my fears when we returned to Paris.

My husband cut me off, "Oh, she got into it, we had fun, didn't we?"

I always said to myself, why upset him? And I used this basic axiom as an excuse not to say anything. If I'd resisted right away, would things have changed? What he liked couldn't displease me, and I quickly realized that any discussion would be at best sterile, at worst a source of conflict.

Verbally, he was already often aggressive. I'd noticed the way he addressed his parents, even though they were very nice, and it shocked me.

My mother-in-law would sometimes sigh and say, "Ah, he always had a temper!..." I think she confused personality with bad temper.

He had practically no friends, apart from a certain Gérard, a colleague who was his regular and willing whipping boy. How many times did I see him throw Gérard out and call him back two days later as if nothing had happened?

This was one of its hallmarks, the erasure of the tape.

He could wake me up in the morning insulting me because I'd forgotten to buy sugar, scream, break the sugar bowl and force me to clean up. Then he'd go take his shower and come back, smiling, relaxed, friendly. If I had the bad taste to refer to his outbursts of anger, he'd shout even louder: "What's the matter with you, pouting all the time? It's unbearable!"

The watchword with him was "Shh, he'll get mad!"

I can still see my mother-in-law putting a finger to her lips to command silence, as she could feel her son's nervous tension filling the room.

Nervous tension: that feeling of anguish that gripped me for over ten years, accompanying my every gesture, my every word, with the mad fear of suddenly seeing his expression turn into an angry rictus, his gestures become jerky.

I never, ever knew what would trigger his rage... And afterwards, I felt guilty, repeating to myself: "You shouldn't have said or done this..."

My neighbor was an elderly lady who had known my husband when he was a child. She was sometimes absent and forgot her keys outside. One day, she stopped me on the stairs: "Is he nice to you? Doesn't he throw tantrums anymore? Because I've heard a lot of shouting, and I've seen broken crockery fall out of the window... You look so sweet, so kind... Don't let it get to you," she whispered.

These words made me uncomfortable. I mentioned it to my mother-in-law, who exclaimed: "Oh, she's a bit of a spoilt brat! Of course, my son was difficult as a child, but that's all over now, he's as nice as can be... "

Yet she, too, caught us arguing. As long as I was married, she took my side and did her best to calm her son down. When he spoke curtly to me, she'd say "Come on!" with a shocked expression, but I think she was more afraid that I wouldn't be able to stand her son. He'd leave, slamming the door, and come back a few hours later, all smiles, with flowers, an invitation to a restaurant, a kiss. And she'd give me a knowing look, like: "You see, you just have to wait it out..."

That was the difficulty. This alternation of pleasant moments and unheard-of violence.

Sometimes we'd spend weeks getting on well together, making plans, laughing and talking to each other.

At times like this, I would tell myself that there was no reason for it, that he could be the best of husbands and that I should be patient and wait it out.

And then it started all over again. I hadn't understood that it was impulsive, that my words were just a pretext to trigger his exasperation and that I wasn't the cause of his mood swings. He was like a spinning top, twisted on himself, spinning and spinning until he was dizzy. In the end, he often didn't know where his anger had come from, and sometimes even cried in a fit of rage, at which point I could sense that he was suffering.

I'd comfort him, hug him like a child, and sometimes he'd be as downcast as if he didn't know where he was anymore. I'd reassure myself that he needed me, that I was soothing him, that with time I'd get the hang of it and he'd have fewer crises...

At other times, when the anger didn't evaporate, when I feared a blow given in a sudden gesture of anger, I would ask him to forgive me, imagining that this would calm him down. Saying: "I'm sorry, excuse me", proving to him that he was right, that I was wrong and, above all, that I recognized his supremacy. But sometimes, forgiveness wasn't enough, and what followed were laborious explanations in which he asked me to admit my wrongdoings at length; I ended up losing my patience and getting angry in my turn. He'd lose his temper and we'd both scream.

Because I wasn't that gentle. I was also thinking of a tactic, telling myself that resisting him could also force him to realize the point of discord we had reached. It was a bad idea: the more I shouted, the more I resisted, the more he gloated, then took the liberty of telling me I was just being hysterical...

Even then, I was lucid enough to realize that something was wrong. But I told myself that if our relationship was shaky, I

Chapter 2

could certainly fix things. With patience, love and getting to know him better.

I too was becoming a manipulator. I knew what words to use to hurt her with a smile, to be indifferent to her anger, to get her to do what I wanted by feigning contradictory desire.

If I wanted to invite a friend over on a Saturday, I'd say:

"Alice wanted to see me, but I told her you were tired on weekends, you had other things to do than see people, so maybe we'll see each other one evening...

- What? What right have you got to manage invitations like that? Saying I'm tired on top of it!... It's crazy! Tell him to come for lunch on Saturday. In fact, I'll give him a call..."

My friend was surprised and thought I had a charming, friendly husband who accepted his wife's friends...

I became complicated, anticipating his reactions the better to counter them, and above all, I didn't talk about it, feeling confused that all this wasn't quite right. What wonder if, years later, my friends didn't believe me and reminded me how kind and caring my husband had been?

Silence and withdrawal start very early in this type of relationship. Because I wanted to keep this relationship. I didn't want to see the inevitable, I didn't want to admit it.

Like so many other women in this situation, I took part in the spiral, weaving the web of my own trap, working day after day to tighten the unhealthy bonds of contained violence around us. This is what I call the second phase, the first being stupefaction and astonishment when violence explodes for the first time.

This second phase is one of denial.

Life was normal, outbursts of anger or verbal violence were legitimate because they were exceptional, in short, everything was fine and I, like so many women in my situation, strove to give those around me the illusion of a perfect life.

First, I'd been a coward, preferring the comfort of a risky married life to the rough edges of life. Then, I'd been too proud to admit that I'd made a serious mistake and that my life was a fiasco. So I lied to everyone, starting with myself.

What's more, I still believed in that love - it wasn't there, but I thought I could get it there. And when you still believe in Prince Charming, you think you can see him behind every toad!

One day, he was offered a job in Morocco and managed to get me hired too. I was delighted. Living so close to my parents was a catalyst for arguments, and I thought it would be good to get away from them.

A few months after our wedding, in the summer, we moved to Tangier. It was the only happy period of our marriage.

We took the camper van by road to Spain, while the move followed.

I remember those increasingly hot lands, the evenings in lively, colorful towns, and at the end, the sea, the boat that dropped us off in Ceuta. I felt like my life was finally taking shape, I was going to work at a radio station in Tangier, Medi1, and I'd really be doing the job I loved. I was lucky to be hired, and my husband, who wouldn't have stood for me not working, seemed happy: "I don't want a wife at home, I'd feel like I was living with my mother!"

The radio team, made up of French and Moroccans, proved to be very friendly. However, my husband soon got into an argument with almost all the editorial staff!

He always criticized me, but I felt he was more relaxed, away from his parents, especially his mother. In fact, the only time we

quarreled during the year we spent in Tangier was when his parents
came to stay for a few days. He had a fusional and conflicting
relationship with his mother, and an odd one with his father. In
fact, both his parents feared him, and he had come to realize that
when they were around, the world revolved around him. But over
there, in Morocco, we were at home, I was no longer at his place.
We had a large apartment facing the bay, with a beautiful terrace,
and the sunsets were marvellous.

It was in front of the ocean one day that we decided to have a
baby. I wanted to wait a while, but he was in a hurry and wanted
children. Looking back, I wonder why, since he couldn't stand
them afterwards! I think it was a social image, the fact of having a
family reassured and comforted him.

I had a miscarriage in Tangier. The child was almost full term and
I was very unhappy about it. He didn't understand. In his eyes, this
unborn child wasn't real yet. It was Amina, our fatma, who looked
after and comforted me.

"Allah is great," she'd tell me, "if he wants, next year you'll have
a boy!"

But he, I had to learn, never stayed in one place for long.

Less than a year after our arrival, he already wanted to return.
Everyone had come to dislike him, and people were telling me in
the corridors of the radio station that they hated him.

Some of my friends took me aside and said: "But you've got to
reason with him, you can see he's alienating everyone...."

I defended him: he had his reasons, and his remarks were
professionally relevant.

I thought he reserved his mood swings for me, but I discovered
that he was exactly the same at work. He had his faces, the people

he liked, the people he couldn't stand. He himself would not tolerate anyone's annoyance.

One day, one of his young colleagues came looking for me, very upset. I was preparing my show, working on documentation and looking for music to illustrate the two hours I spent on air every day. I loved this job, which was part animation, part journalism, and that period was a great professional opportunity for me. But he managed to spoil everything: "Listen, come on, your husband's overly upset and I'm afraid it's going to end badly... At one point I was afraid he was going to come to blows with the financial director...".

I put down my work and tumbled down the stairs to the reporters' desk. He was screaming and two other people were staring at him, dumbfounded. I approached him and he calmed down. The others left the office and I stayed beside him, working.

Like an unruly child, my presence soothed and reassured him. I assured him he was right, that I understood him, and little by little, he became almost normal again.

In the evening, we returned home, walking down the boulevard de Tanger as the stars lit up one by one in the sky. He said to me: "Your presence does me a world of good, you're the only one who understands me, you know how to give me peace...".

He'd gone back to being as nice as can be and, stupidly, I imagined myself bringing him well-being.

The next day, in the radio studios, he was cheerful and playful. Everyone looked at me with bewilderment. I glanced at them to make sure they didn't hint.

Everything was back to normal, he was charming and, for me, that was the most important thing. I even came to resent those who held a grudge against him. I said to myself: "They could make an effort, they're going to ruin everything! I'd already lost sight of the fact that it was he who was ruining everything.

The persuasiveness of a manipulator who made me believe that he was a charming man and that it was up to me, up to us, to keep him that way...

Any drift was attributable to the outside world, and mainly to me.

The team had got into the habit of coming to see me to sort out relationship problems caused by my husband. I think, deep down, I was flattered, I felt I existed, I had a social role. I was pretty much in control of the situation. I defused conflicts and felt that everything was fine.

But he eventually took umbrage.

One day, one of the station managers, after a big argument with him, ends up telling him: "Listen, we're keeping you on because of your wife, who's charming and nice, but if you leave, nobody will miss you...".

That same evening, he made a scene of unprecedented violence: "It's all your fault, I can see through your game, you're trying to get me out, but poor thing, who do you think you are? You're here because of me, you're nothing without me, you're paid in dirhams, you have no future here, if I leave you'll lose everything...".

It was true. I had agreed to be paid in local currency with a Moroccan contract. As a result, we lived on my salary and he saved all of his. I thought this was a logical arrangement: he was better paid, it was better for him to be the one saving, and I thought the money belonged to us (a grave error I later learned to my cost).

And then it was true, it was he who had negotiated this contract for me and this line on my CV was a very positive point. I thought I was ungrateful. I ended up crying. I thought he was right, that it was he who had offered me the job, that I'd probably pushed too hard to compensate for his attitude and, as a result, it was my fault that people preferred me to him.

I was responsible for his failure, I stood between him and the others, I begged his forgiveness and, at that moment, I really thought I'd ruined everything, without even realizing it. Eventually he calmed down and decided to go back to France. I was disappointed when he told me that he had withdrawn from his contract. Now that he was available, he could go back to his TV job. My position, my job, was not even discussed. It was understood that it wasn't important. He was to reproach me for it later: "You're not capable of making savings, look, I've managed to put tens of thousands of francs aside!"

On the evening of our departure, I received gifts and tokens of affection that warmed my heart, but which I carefully concealed. He left his office overnight and never came back to say goodbye.

My boss received me alone. He was a generous, intelligent man in his fifties: "You know, Marianne," he said, "if you want to stay here, I can arrange your contract..."

I declined. And for the second time, I steered the course of my destiny by chaining my life to that of a man who wasn't doing me any good. I might have joined the Société financière de radiodiffusion (SOFIRAD), I might have stayed in Morocco? I had no children. But I was married. I couldn't see myself staying on my own in Morocco. For me, the separation would have been a failure and I wasn't ready. And then I told myself that he needed me, that I couldn't abandon him.

For a long time, this was my credo, a sign of my importance. I felt useful, necessary; it was really clever...

The trip home was a sad one. I'd begged him not to come back to his apartment, but he'd told me we were lucky his parents had kept him for us.

"It's temporary, I promise, we'll look for something else later..."

On the boat back to Sète, I got seasick, and that irritated him. When we got to Sète, he left me with the camper van. He had a business appointment and thought I could make the whole trip on my own while he took the plane.

I traveled over a thousand kilometers to get back to Paris.

I had left Tangier, the beautiful city on the Mediterranean, our apartment by the sea, a job I liked, faithful friends, and I had lost my baby.

The future, in that sense, looked a lot less rosy.

I landed back in the apartment I'd always hated. My mother-in-law was radiant, reunited with her son, and I ended up burying my dreams of a home of our own... We had this apartment, in a beautiful neighborhood, rent-free: my dreams of distance seemed like those of a spoiled child.

Two days after our return, we unpacked the boxes. Methodically, one by one, he put all the furniture back where it had been a year and a half earlier.

I was sick of seeing an apartment that wasn't mine take shape before my eyes. I was tired, irritated. I tried to open a box with a knife, but couldn't. He took it out of my hand, angrily. He grabbed it out of my hand, furiously. When I tried to protest, he stared into my eyes. In one fell swoop, the blade of the knife cut my forearm. Blood splattered onto the cardboard, he dropped the knife and in a second, his face changed. He took me in his arms: "I'm sorry, I'm sorry," he stammered, "I didn't mean to..."

My arm was bleeding badly, and he decided to take me to the Boucicaut hospital in the 15th arrondissement. I stayed there several times afterwards.

Before leaving, he rang his parents' doorbell and said: "Marianne's hurt, I'm taking her to the emergency room...".

Although the blood was still flowing, it was no longer painful. The knife hadn't reached the flesh. My husband looked deeply shaken, and I told myself that he had understood how serious and violent his outbursts could be. I thought he'd learned his lesson and wouldn't do it again. What a mistake! It must have been the first of many violent acts.

He bravely held my hand as I was stitched up:

"How did you do your count?" scolded the intern.

And my husband replied:

- Oh, you know, Doctor, she's such a klutz!"

I was crying. I don't even know if it was pain, anger, shame or guilt.

I should have told him right away that it was over, that I wouldn't tolerate his actions anymore. But I was already conditioned. And at that moment, he looked really contrite, I didn't want to add fuel to the fire.

I know today that you have to leave at the first violent gesture, at the first slap. Because others will always follow. But I also know that, most of the time, that's not possible. You need to stand back to see the outcome of the scenario. At the time, like a fly caught in a spider's web, you struggle, before realizing that there's no other solution but to stay still.

As we left the hospital, he kissed me and took me to a restaurant. I felt like I was stepping back into a rut I'd struggled to get out of. But I still believed things could change, evolve. I believed that he had understood the seriousness of his actions, the folly of his behavior.

I said to him one day:

"Listen, we have everything to be happy, happiness is in our hands, why are you bent on destroying it?"

He replied in a hateful tone:

- I don't care about your happiness, I don't care about being happy, you don't know! You have a narrow view of life if all you care about is being happy!"

I was flabbergasted. I'd put it down to anger, but it was really what he was thinking. His aim wasn't happiness, nor was it to make me happy. On the contrary, he delighted in conflict, rage and resentment.

After that first stab, a page had been turned.

From insults, mockery and psychological pressure, he moved on to beatings and physical violence.

Here again, when I think back to my state of mind at the time, I'm flabbergasted by so much confusion. I had lost my first baby, and I was focused on the project of a new pregnancy. Since I'd failed, my whole focus was on bringing a new life to term. He wanted a child too, it was the only project that seemed to relax him. I thought, if he wants a child, it means he still believes in us, it means he loves me.

Strangely enough, I didn't ask myself whether I loved him... No, I thought: a child, a family, is bound to be happy. I'd been happy as a child, with my brothers and sister, and I believed that if I restored the balance between parents and children, he would flourish. But while I was going along with my idea, he was thinking mainly about how to bind me to him even more. He sensed that he had often overstepped the mark, that I could still leave, a child, he thought, would hold her back. Many men and women believe that children tie a spouse down, when in fact they more often than not separate them, and even a united couple can experience the ordeal. I once knew an unemployed woman who left a violent husband with her four children and slept in her car for eight days before finding a home. How many have chosen uncertainty and hardship over a life of drama and beatings?

At the time, I believed that a child would normalize our relationship. We shared the same ideas about education, the same values. We came from similar backgrounds, and I think that reassured me. I could see that he could be different, nice and pleasant. I believed that all we had to do was create the right conditions for him to stay that way. He wanted a baby as much as I did, and I was convinced that a child would give him a taste for a serene life.

I should have understood that his perversity of character was tinged with a sickly jealousy: this child would take his attention from me, I would devote time to him, yet my time was unquestionably devoted to him. He saw himself as the eternal victim of the whole world, which constantly owed him reparations.

One day, it will be his children he makes suffer. But I was blinding myself trying to get pregnant.

He was nearly 35 and kept saying: "I don't want to be an old father, look, I had an old father, and he never played soccer with me, I suffered for it…"

He wanted a son, who had to look like him. So I did my utmost to comply with his wishes, with the help of Mother Nature, who didn't let me down this time.

CHAPTER 3

We had a son, Jean, two years later. It was the happiest day of my life. Thirty years later, I can still see the joy and emotion when he was born.

His son is the only one of his children he has ever seen born. As for his daughters, he managed to avoid them every time. He hated hospitals. In fact, he would have left straight away, but an imposing midwife handed him the gown and mask: he didn't dare refuse. Thanks to the epidural, I didn't suffer too much, and I remember talking to the nurse about the Falklands War - a very topical subject. Shortly before delivery, he managed to utter an enormity that left the midwife stunned: "Well, maybe I'll go and have some lunch... No, because you're obviously lying down, you don't realize it, but I've been standing up all this time!"

His son announced himself at the same time, and survived by skipping a meal (which he was to refer to as a heroic act on his part).

At last he was happy, fulfilled!

Or so I thought. Because the trouble started as soon as I got back from the maternity ward.

I remember arriving home. It was May, raining and gray. I had the baby in my arms, and I tried to feed him, sitting on the sofa. When I got up, I saw that the diaper was ill-fitting and that bright yellow excrement was dripping down my legs and onto the carpet. I stood up, my husband looked at me, and then I burst into tears. This was my first child and I was very tired. Already in the maternity ward, I sometimes cried from exhaustion. I could see that my tears were unsettling him. He turned around in the room, helpless, forgetting to cry out, all disconcerted. He whispered half-heartedly: "What am I going to do if you don't make it?"

It was like a shock, and I pulled myself together. I said to myself: "You're ridiculous, come on, he's counting on you; they both need you", and this idea galvanized me. Why did I need to be needed so much? To this day, I still find it hard when I feel that I'm not helping the people around me; I feel like I'm useless. However, I eventually learned to get out of this role of hyper-responsible, big man of the universe, I learned to show my limits.

But in those days, it was impossible. Whenever my husband felt I was at my wits' end, in trouble, he either took the opportunity to overwhelm me, or panicked.

My son had become the center of my life. He was annoyed by this, but he also quickly understood how to make the most of it.

One day, in the kitchen, for some trifling matter, I dared to upset him. He said to me:

"If you keep this up, I'm going to get the kid and leave him here in the kitchen....

- He's asleep, why do you want to go and get him?

- Well, he'll wake up and see you crying as usual!"

I calmed down and he finally forgot about it. I was terrified. I understood that he wanted to involve the little one in our arguments, to use him to muzzle me, to shut me up.

The next day, he bought a state-of-the-art stroller to take his son for a walk. He took good care of him, bathing him and bottle-feeding him. He was an attentive father and seemed happy to have this child.

But as soon as I upset him, he'd pick him up in his crib and scream, scream, scream, with the baby in his arms. I soon realized that I shouldn't try to take him away from him. I left the room and locked myself in the bathroom. He would immediately put the child down. And comfort him if he cried.

I concluded that it was my presence that catalyzed his violence. From there, I felt perpetually guilty... I told myself that I was annoying him, that I didn't know how to handle him... I was on the lookout for the slightest gesture or word that might irritate him. I was exhausted, as much by the baby, the throes of childbirth, as by his presence.

He felt that I was spending too much time with him, that I was holding him too much. Like all infants, my son needed my presence, but any time spent with my child seemed to him to be deducted from the time he was entitled to.

Anyway, it was time for this to stop and he ordered me to get back to work.

I got a job at a specialist weekly.

Jean was put in the care of a very nice lady a stone's throw from our house, and his father went to pick him up every evening. I cried a lot at first: leaving my 4-month-old baby all day was tearing my heart out. He would say to me, not without reason: "Well, you've got to get back into it, because in this job you'll soon be forgotten, and you're not going to turn into a wife either...".

I think to myself today that, thanks to his insistence, I finally had a rich professional life. Who knows? With a more accommodating husband, I might have let myself go, taken parental leave and, when the time came, found it even harder to leave.

I think he loved his son, but what he couldn't stand was the three-way relationship. He didn't want to share me and felt that the child was taking up too much of my time. In the evenings, I'd rush to hug Jean, to play with him, to touch him. He would follow me step by step, talking to me, asking me in an annoyed tone: "Are you listening to me?"

He kept fairly flexible hours and came home early. On the few evenings he was on call, I could breathe. Jean and I would spend a delightfully serene evening together, and then I would have a late dinner with my husband. Everything was going well. I was all ears, all available to listen to him, and that's what he wanted. He never asked me any questions, or else he demanded a detailed account of the little one's day, which he used to criticize me: "Did you go to the park? What time did you go? Three-thirty! But that's much too late, the damp falls early... What do you mean, he was asleep? But he shouldn't sleep so much, what did you feed him?"

Fortunately, he didn't listen to the answers and more often than not quickly turned his monologue to the subject he was most passionate about: Him. I had a magic formula when I saw him warming up: "And you?"

This simple question immediately brought him back to his exclusive focus. I was thinking about something else, punctuating his sentences with "Ah! Yes? Good!" which put him back in the saddle for a few minutes of logorrhea.

My son must have been 7 years old when one day he exclaimed to his father: "But Dad, you haven't yet understood that when Mom says, 'Yes, yes, that's very good', she's not listening to you!"

He was taken aback.

My husband's egocentric personality prevented him from finding his place. I knew something had to be done, but I felt helpless, guilty either for not giving him enough attention or for neglecting my son.

"It's normal, all fathers react like that, they find it hard to accept that the child has priority, try to devote more time to your husband, entrust the little one to him, go away together...".

So I left Jean at my mother's for a week and off we went to Senegal.

My daughter, Pauline, was conceived there, on a white sandy beach.

My husband was beaming, saying he finally had a family, and I was happy to see him happy. He managed to get the apartment above ours and started work on a duplex. He had plans, his work was progressing, he was going off on reports and coming back with memories, stories he knew how to tell, and I thought the bad days were over.

And so it was, for a few beautiful months, but unfortunately his father died suddenly following heart surgery. He was 73 years old. He was a very nice man, who let his son bully him without saying too much. He was delighted to have a grandson and he was really good to me. I think he was aware of his son's character, and often said to me: "My little Marianne, you're going to need patience...".

When he died, my husband had a breakdown that I didn't recognize at the time. He regretted his fights with his father. My father-in-law, gentle and charming, was not at all the kind of father he would have needed. On the contrary, he would have needed to be very firm and set limits. He had been beating his father since the age of 15, my mother-in-law told me, laughing. I was horrified, but she seemed to find the situation funny: "Oh, it was hectic at home, you know!"

In fact, my husband used to get a kick out of it too. He used to tell stories of how he'd broken a window in the living room chasing his father, how he'd thrown all the papers from his father's desk out of the window and sent his mother crawling across the ground-floor lawn to retrieve them. These memories of conflict seemed to be the only moments of his childhood that he remembered with pleasure, almost with pride. It was hard for me to understand, but I didn't want to give an opinion. I told myself that all families had their setbacks, that it was all in the past. In short, I didn't want to dig into it either...

I still remember the morning we received a phone call from the nursing home. I was dressing Jean in his little bed and I heard them shout: "What? What? But that's not possible... Wait, I'll put you through to my wife..." He was shocked and said, "Listen, you go ahead, I've got appointments..."

I realized that he couldn't face reality. When life hit him head-on, he suffered from the unacceptable idea that he had no control over anything and that the elements were beyond his control. As soon as his omnipotence was held in check by the vagaries of life (whether it was the weather thwarting his plans or the death of a loved one), he collapsed in shock.

I was the one who recognized the body, closed the coffin, brought my mother-in-law home and took care of all the burial paperwork.

"I can't stand hospitals and cemeteries," he told me.

At the cemetery, it was me again who climbed into the van, to accompany the body with my tearful mother-in-law. It was February, the weather was freezing, and I could feel my mother-in-law trembling as she said: "I'm all alone now...".

Neither her daughter, too busy counting the inheritance, nor her son were around her. I felt she was so unhappy. My husband, on the other hand, was absent-minded, with that look I knew him for when he wanted to provoke a conflict.

He burst out when he returned to his mother's house and saw that she had kept my stepfather's things spread out on the bed. Disregarding his mother's cries, he grabbed them and threw them in the garbage can, then locked himself in his room. "Don't worry, we'll pick them up later," I whispered in her ear. She sighed, sobbing contentedly: "Yes, yes, I know..."

We were linked, she by the grief of having lost her husband whom she adored, I by the worry of dealing with a temperamental husband. But then I realized that she knew her son, that she often feared his temper; like me, she was used to it and did the best she could. He was her son, she loved him. He was my husband and I had to help him, even if I could feel that the love between us was evaporating with every argument.

In the months that followed, he became withdrawn. He cried every night. His work suffered and he took a sick leave. At that point, we should have helped him, encouraged him to seek help. But my second baby was due and all I could think about was the birth. My mother-in-law rejoiced at the event, it was the only thing that pulled her out of her grief, but he was sinking. The fact that he was calmer was enough for me; I was happy that he was leaving me alone, that there was less shouting.

My daughter was born in Normandy, with my mother-in-law who, as always, was very kind to me. I think that deep down, she was already old, she realized that her son wasn't well, that he had a temper bordering on the pathological, and she relieved herself by being very considerate with me. She was afraid I'd leave him, afraid I'd end up with her son on my hands. "It's true," she would tell me, "his first fiancée died in a car accident, and he was really shaken up...".

I was amazed, he'd never told me about it! He had an ability to bury the traumas that were bound to explode in his brain one day... Certainly he hadn't been helped by his family environment, in which we didn't talk to each other; and then again, in those days we didn't care much about child psychology.

His godfather, a first cousin of his father's, would later tell me that my husband had spent time in a Swiss nursing home at the age of 15. One day, when he was in ninth grade, he came home from school saying he wasn't going to class anymore. What had happened? No one knew, and no one tried to find out. He stayed at home, more or less lying on his bed, from February to September. Just once, he confided in me that one of the fathers had made an inappropriate gesture towards him. He hadn't told anyone about it, preferring to wait until he was dismissed.

Even then, his parents were careful not to upset him... It was his godfather who finally took matters into his own hands, diagnosing depression, advising removal from the family environment and sending the child to Switzerland.

My husband once told me that he had very fond memories of the school. He'd made friends there, they imposed limits and rules on him, and deep down he needed them. But then his mother fell ill...

Perhaps his determination to separate me, to keep me away from the children, was dictated by the memory of too strong a relationship with his mother? He had a vague feeling that she had been harmful, and held a grudge. Hence his constant bullying of her, as if she had to pay for something. "I know you mean well, but believe me, you mustn't spoil the children too much..." he said to me one day. What did he mean by spoil?

This complicated, fusional bond with her mother only worsened over time.

When Pauline was born, I took a few months' leave, but he, distraught at his father's death and no doubt undermined by the regret of their incessant arguments, became increasingly antisocial and temperamental, and ended up slamming the door on his job. Very quickly, to avoid remorse, he rewrote the story of his father's death as he knew how: he had never quarreled with his father, who had a heart condition. On the contrary, he'd been protecting him, but the doctors had misdiagnosed him and put in a pacemaker too late. Then, on his way home, he had his wallet snatched from him in the street by a thug, and that's what had caused his death. I was surprised, years later, to hear him say:

"My father was murdered...

- ???

- But yes, it's that guy, that thief who caused the heart attack, he hasn't recovered from it!"

His father died three months after this incident, in a convalescent home... But there was no point in discussing his version, it was the one that suited him and any discussion was dangerous.

I went back to work, and he looked after the children. It wasn't a solution; he didn't have the patience and felt diminished by staying at home. He was becoming increasingly irascible. One evening, I came home from work, my daughter was playing in her playpen and her brother was watching TV. He was alone. He'd gone to buy tobacco and returned twenty minutes later. The children were 1 and 3...

Alone with them he couldn't cope, and I had to hire a young girl for the day. He couldn't stand her. He fired one after the other of the girls I hired...

In spite of everything, he really looked after his daughter, Pauline, with whom he forged a special bond, almost a genuine attachment. He used to say that she looked like him, that she was on his side (which was true, by the way). This was obviously a great quality and a blessing for the child, he liked to imply. In fact, he once said to me: "You're lucky, after all, the three of them are more on my side...".

I knew he couldn't be satisfied with this domestic life for long. Without telling him, I organized dinners and more or less chance meetings so that he could get back to work, or at least get a few leads.

Eventually he found work again, on assignments in the French overseas territories for a few months.

He was delighted. The job suited him: no routine, three- or four-month stints. He barely had time to argue with everyone before he was back; besides, he loved his job and was happy to share it. All his trainees, his students when he taught, adored him. One of his editors was to say to me later: "It was crazy, your husband, the first eight days everyone adored him, and then everything went downhill and everyone came to my office begging me to fire him... He was incapable of stable behavior. I assure you that three months is his long limit..."

In fact, despite all these missions, he was never granted tenure, and for good reason!

Nobody wanted to put the wolf in the sheepfold.

But our relationship was less tense. I had my life and my work. When he came back, he was happy to see the kids and me again, and I made every effort, knowing that his departure date was fixed.

One day, however, when my grandmother was visiting me, he returned from a trip in the middle of the afternoon. From the look on his face, I knew something was wrong. We were having coffee and he stood in front of us, pointing at my grandmother: "What the hell is she doing here? I'd like to have some peace and quiet when I get home!"

The poor thing was stunned. I was furious and said to him curtly: "Listen, go and get some rest and above all calm down, what's wrong with talking like that?" He kicked Pauline's bassinet and she started to cry. My grandmother got up and said: "Well, listen, I'm going to go now, my darling...".

I grabbed my kids and pulled on their jackets. We descended the stairs four by four, leaving him to rant and rave, and I drove my grandmother back to the metro. I tried to downplay the incident, to say that he must have been upset at work, but she wasn't fooled. It was she who begged me, a few years later in her hospital bed: "Leave him, darling, or he'll kill you...".

A year after Pauline, I lost another child. Six months pregnant, I developed an infection and broke my water. It was nighttime, I felt the liquid coming out, and I knew right away that it was serious. I got up, called a cab and woke my husband. He had to stay with the sleeping children and wasn't overly alarmed.

When I called him back a few hours later to tell him they were keeping me, he started whining: "But what am I going to do all alone with the kids?"

Mom came every day to look after them.

I was determined to lie still for the next few months, so that the baby wouldn't be born too soon. I didn't want to lose him.

Alas, the baby died *in utero* and the delivery was awful.

I cried so much, with loneliness, sorrow and disappointment.

I think that's when I stopped loving him.

When that baby was expelled from my womb, he took with him the love I still had for my husband. He hadn't come to assist me, and when he arrived in my room, when I was already in tears, he managed to make me cry harder. "It's all your fault," he said, "if only you'd been paying attention, but you're obviously not listening. If that little boy is dead, you've only got yourself to blame, you're irresponsible...".

I cried so hard that finally the head nurse arrived and threw him out, telling him to come back when he'd calmed down and had something more comforting to say to me!

He left in a huff.

Today, people say that mothers should be allowed to hold their dead child in their arms for a while, to give them time to say goodbye and mourn. It wasn't yet common practice, but I was lucky: the doctors were overwhelmed and I was left alone at the time of expulsion. I was at the end of my tether and had been suffering for hours. Every now and then, a nurse would pop in to make sure I was okay. I felt as if life was going to leave me. Suddenly, a terrible pain split me in two. I stood up. Just one push and I had between my legs a tiny baby, all black, cyanotic, with hair stuck to his head, like his brother, and sucking his thumb.

I stroked his head, gently, and then lifted him up. His cord was all bloody. I held him close to me. A nurse's aide came in, a woman from Martinique, and she shouted: "But, madame, what are you up to?"

She took my baby from me and laid me on the bed. The doctor appeared and said he was swamped and had to put me to sleep. I turned my head and woke up as if from a nightmare. I was on a stretcher, the orderly was checking my drip and I said:

"What are we going to do with my baby? It was a boy, I wanted to call him Quentin...

- Yes, well ma'am, you mustn't think about that, stillborn babies are cremated, come on ma'am, he's like a little angel now, you mustn't cry..."

She gently stroked my head and tucked me in maternally. When the stretcher-bearer arrived, she said to him in her accent: "Take it easy on that lady, she's had her baby, it's to twiste...".

I was left alone, walled in by my grief. My husband was certainly sad too, but we couldn't, didn't know how to listen to our grief. He was reproachful, while I shielded myself with indifference or aggression. I know today that he couldn't console me, he had no access to compassion. Years later, Jean would say to me: "No, but Mom, you don't understand, Dad doesn't have the application, he can't love, that's all, he wasn't programmed to...".

It took me a long time to recover. I took refuge in my children, who were my greatest joy. I wanted to get pregnant again, as a revenge, as a victory over life.

For the next two years, I was obsessed with the desire to have a child. I wanted to achieve a goal, to create a family, no matter with whom. I had my job, the kids; he had his, which was a bit chaotic because he was always slamming the door, but I didn't care. I went on vacation without him, I had my activities with the kids and I avoided him as much as possible.

When I conceived my youngest, I was overjoyed. She was my baby, and I had wanted her so much, even more than the others. Is that why she arrived two weeks late? I was so afraid of losing her!

His father was on a mission in Guadeloupe. He returned for the birth and left two months later. He had barely seen her. My little girl, with her red puff, her blue eyes, she was beautiful.

He looked after them less than he did the older ones, leaving each time for periods of three to four months. That suited me. This child was mine, I felt invincible, I was transmitting my strength and energy to her, in the absence of a calm family life. I felt that destiny would be exceptional for her, that everything would work out for her. Her father would never be able to touch her, never, I would protect her.

With my Dina, a milestone had been reached. I was no longer concerned with preserving the family or calming down crises, I stood up like a she-wolf to anyone who dared to harm my little ones. The two eldest had been through it all, they'd had their share of fights. I swore to myself that things would be different for my last one. I would no longer let myself be pushed around. I would no longer compose, I would resist.

My strength came from my children. But circumstances had also changed. He was often away, for long weeks at a time, and I had time to regain my courage, to catch my breath, to analyze the situation, to open my eyes. Because habit creates submission, and everyday life makes the atrocious seem normal. Habituality allows for effective strategies that become like a weapon you wield without realizing it.

Was he shouting? I left the room. Did he get loud? Depending on the time of day, I'd get the kids dressed, we'd go to school early, to the park, to a friend's house, or even to the local café. He'd get angry all by himself, and I could feel his anger getting closer? So I'd pick up the phone and pretend to call my mother, in a cheerful voice; he'd be afraid she'd hear and end up grumbling. Was he suggesting an outing, an idea? I was careful not to be enthusiastic if I liked it...

After two and a half years, I was organized and imagined that everything was fine. My life was full of pitfalls, which I patiently circumvented with one fixed idea in mind: protecting the children. I think that when their father was around, we never spent half a day at home: they had activities, the toy library, judo, piano; I went to my parents' house, invented a thousand essential outings...

But one day, between two missions, he stayed with us for almost two months. It was hell. He'd yell at the kids for anything and everything, and hit me at the slightest annoyance.

One evening, we were expecting friends and I was preparing dinner. He circled around me, turning down the fire I'd lit, stirring in the pots, shouting at the children, pushing the table I'd set. I finally got carried away:

"But are you going to leave me alone at last!

- But you're not making any sense, look at that, those beans are already overcooked!"

He was screaming like a madman. He wanted to slam the kitchen glass door, but I stretched out my arm to hold him back. My hand went through the glass and a piece of glass cut the extensor tendon of my finger...

Blood spurted out as our guests arrived. He immediately became agitated, panicking: "She's so clumsy, ah là là!"

I spent the evening with my hand wrapped in a tea towel that was blushing red. At around eleven o'clock, one of our friends suggested we take me to hospital.

I had to be operated on during the night. Once again I was crying, out of helplessness and anger at myself.

He picked me up the next day with a big bouquet of flowers. I should have told him that his actions were insane, that I'd had enough of his perpetual mood swings. But he was kind, soothing: "You're too stressed," he said, "look, I'm trying to help you and you're getting yourself into a state that's impossible!" I knew it wasn't my fault. That his behavior was unacceptable. I should have told my family, filed a complaint. But I wasn't ready. When I got home, the children were playing peacefully and he'd prepared dinner.

This was a constant in our relationship. He could be adorable, thoughtful, kind to the kids, and the next minute slapping Jean for dropping his timbale, yelling at his mother for going upstairs to read the news, and breaking a stack of plates because the mail was late.

When I came home from work, I could feel a lump forming in my throat. I would mentally pray that he wouldn't be there. I'd quickly dismiss the young girl who was looking after them and take care of the children. The baths, homework and dinner had to be done before he arrived. If I was upstairs and heard the front door slam, my blood would freeze.

More often than not, I'd hear the cry, "Whose business is this lying around?"

My things and those of the children - coats, shoes, schoolbags - had to be stored out of his sight, in the closet. Only his things were allowed on the coat rack, and his shoes in the hallway.

He would go upstairs and enter the bathroom: "Figure-toi que..."

He'd go off into a monologue about his day. In the best of cases, he'd follow me, grumbling, and I'd carry on doing what I had to do, nodding from distance. There was no need to ask him to wait, to go into the living room, to give me a few moments. No, I had to listen to her right away.

When he was in a bad mood, he would shout and insult me. I'd leave the kids to fend for themselves and isolate myself with him, trying to calm him down.

My son quickly learned to understand his father's moods.

With a glance between us, he understood. I'd go with his father to the living room and he'd take over with his sisters. How many times did I see him push the girls to their room, close the door and make them play so they wouldn't irritate their father? How many times, when I'd say, "It's time for school," and we still had half an hour, he'd get everyone dressed in a hurry and be waiting for me at the top of the stairs. He could smell my fear and spot his father's temper tantrums, compressed like a pressure cooker. What a childhood for him! And I still thought it was better for them to be with both parents!

I ignored the latent conflict, the perennial tension at home. I kept telling myself that they had good living conditions, that their father loved them... I still wanted to convince myself that a father is important.

I lost mine when I was 4, and I've always been amazed at how little people in general thought about the role of the father. I know how hard it is to miss him, how the feeling of incompleteness pursues you, especially when you lose your father before you've had a chance to gather memories, start a relationship, create an attachment. I overvalued this role and, even though I had seen my mother cry so much when she was widowed, I had forgotten the most important thing: children need happy parents.

I often heard well-meaning people tell me that losing a father was less painful than losing a mother. I was furious, ulcerated by this judgment, and felt that my grief was being minimized, that the trauma I had suffered was being brushed aside. I thought my children were lucky to have a father, that I couldn't deprive them of that, that it would have been awful. I confused everything.

I thought my children had the right to live with a dad, even if he wasn't ideal: I also convinced myself that he was surely no worse or better than anyone else... I took the bad times and began to think that I might leave one day if things didn't work out, when my children were older. The project was still a blur, an outline, a smoke in the distance in my mind when, really, I couldn't take it anymore. But I thought about it: with every argument, every scene, this future took shape.

I particularly remember one day when we were returning from the country with the little one. He started to get annoyed with me for giving him the wrong directions. Finally, he stopped dead in his tracks, threw me out of the car, stuck the baby in my arms and sped off. I was left in the middle of the countryside, all alone with the little girl.

I walked to the nearest station and bought a ticket to Paris. My little girl must have been 8 months old, but she didn't seem to be worried, just chirping in my arms. Suddenly, she grabbed my neck and gave me her first kiss!

I was moved to tears, at least I'd earned that kiss!

I didn't want to realize the impact of my husband's reactions on my children. Yet when he was away, they were much more enthusiastic. Jean no longer had nightmares, Pauline was less grumpy. One evening, after a violent argument, I went to put Jean to bed and he said to me: "Mum, why are we staying with him?

Deep down, I think I was dreading exactly what happened next. In other words, my husband was able to pretend that he loved his children as long as we were all together. He was capable of fatherly gestures, of taking care of them, because he had his whipping boy, in this case me, on hand. From the day I left, everything fell apart and he was no longer able to love the children. They became instruments of revenge against me. I think I knew things would turn out this way. I was kidding myself, but deep down I was balancing between two possibilities: either live unhappily with him, together, or leave him, knowing that it would probably be worse for the children who would take the blows on the front line, because I wouldn't be there to protect them.

So I waited for them to grow up.

CHAPTER 4

I decided to take my husband to see a doctor specializing in behavioral disorders. I wanted to help him, I thought he could change, he was sick, he just had to get better. Of course, he didn't agree:

"Well, I'm fine, you're the one who's crazy, poor thing, anyone would go crazy living with you!

- It's true, I'm not feeling well, so I'm going to see someone, but it would help if you came with me..."

I made an appointment with a psychiatrist, a professor who had been recommended to me by a friend. I explained to him that I was asking my husband to come for me. Very understanding, he told me that this could indeed be a solution to get my husband to see a psychiatrist.

The professor was astonishing. He understood the problem right away, I think, prescribing mood-regulating medication, while winning her sympathy by listening to her with compassion. He took me out at one point, and my husband agreed to see him again. My husband was almost glad when he left the practice to have resumed an appointment. He said to me, however, "I'm really doing this for you, my poor girl, because otherwise you're not going to make it..."

He would later use the sessions to my disadvantage, explaining at the time of the divorce that it was really me who wasn't well; as proof, I had been obliged to consult, he had just accompanied me... The judge asked me at the time:

"Madam, do you admit that you made these appointments with a neuropsychiatrist for yourself?

- Not exactly, I wanted to bring my husband...

- Has he agreed to accompany you?

- Yes...

- Why?

- I told him I wasn't feeling well...

- So you admit it was for you?

- But no, it was a ploy to get her to come in for a consultation!

- It's a bit far-fetched..."

At best, I was an unbalanced woman whom my husband had taken to the shrink to help, and at worst, a Machiavellian woman who told her gullible husband anything to help him. With him, the truth was never on my side. He always managed to make himself look good, and I felt pathetic. So I doubted everything, especially myself, and kept thinking that I was at fault and that I'd caused all this violence.

The therapy began to show results. He was calmer, with fewer mood swings. He was almost cheerful at times.

But one day, suddenly, he stopped everything. Medication and counseling. It was a descent into hell. He'd wake up in the morning shouting at everyone, or wake me up in the middle of the night; he'd grab the kids, bully his son... I never knew what mood he'd be in at night. I tried to get him to go to the doctor, but he just wouldn't listen. I was driving him crazy, driving him mad.

I returned to the professor, who received me kindly:

"You know, what I'm doing with your husband is necessary, but it's not enough; he has to accept real therapy, he has to accept treatment. He must now understand and admit that he is ill, and unfortunately he's not ready," he explained.

- So what can I do?

He looked at me with great sympathy and said:

- Nothing, endure... Or leave him... You can't cure him..."

Today, we'd probably say he was bipolar. At the time, no one really put his illness into words. He was said to be temperamental and, of course, this word sounded like a negative judgment, which he could only pass on to others.

I could see that my presence was making things worse. As soon as I'd come home, he'd yell at me, reproach me for ten thousand little things, and the situation would degenerate. When he was alone with the kids, on the other hand, he tried to contain himself; I think he was afraid of what he might do. I was his safeguard, and I was there to protect the children and stop him in time.

The more I got between him and the kids, the more he'd lash out and hit or insult me. I couldn't help it, and when I got too heated, I'd send the kids upstairs to their rooms. "You're afraid, but of what, eh? If you're scared, you're guilty..." he'd throw at me. Once the kids were safe, I'd defend myself and yell at him too.

One day, I left him in the lurch, grabbed my coat and went outside. He slammed the door behind me in a rage and I had to stay outside for two hours. I walked the streets, it was winter, it was cold. I thought of my children, I was afraid for them, but I knew he'd be so helpless on his own that he'd calm down and wouldn't hurt them.

When I got home, he'd put them to bed. He was watching TV and didn't say a word to me.

I went into the bathroom and off to bed.

I'd just fallen asleep when he came into the room and turned on the ceiling light: "You think you can just leave and come back like that? Get out of my bed, get the hell out, this isn't your home, it's mine, get out!"

Unleashed, he pulled back the sheets and blankets; he kicked me, and I tried to protect myself as best I could. Finally, I managed to get up and get out of the room. I locked myself in the bathroom. I heard him walking around the room, grumbling in the corridor and then nothing. He'd gone to bed.

Slowly, I made my way to my son's room, lay down beside him without waking him, and tried to sleep.

I woke up early and slipped out of the room to get ready. My eye was swollen and I had a big gash on my cheek. I tried to make up my wounds as best I could. The children got up. Their father was asleep. I had to look after them and take them to school: fortunately, they didn't seem to notice anything.

When I arrived at work, however, my make-up didn't fool anyone. I told a dark story about how I'd fallen down the stairs at night when I got up. I thought, "As long as he only picks on me, I'll be fine, the kids are safe." Nonsense!

This was the beginning of a long series of lies.

I think that over the years, I managed to make everyone around me believe that I was very clumsy. I was often injured, I had sores, bumps, but I was skating, or any other sport, and I put these marks down to falls, of which there were many.

One day, I had to go to hospital for a broken rib. The doctor noticed the marks on my body. My husband had made progress, managing to avoid making marks on his face; from then on, he kicked me in the stomach and twisted my arms.

The doctor looked at me sternly as I gave him my usual speech about ice skating and falls...

"Madame," he said, "I think you should make a complaint..."

I burst into tears. I couldn't stop.

But that evening, when he came home, there were flowers all over the house. He had bathed and fed the children, and chilled champagne.

He threw himself at my feet: "Sorry, sorry... I'm sorry, I promise it won't happen again..."

He became kind and considerate again for a few weeks. We'd make plans, he'd take me out to dinner, he'd look after the kids, and I thought that since he was capable of being so adorable, it must be that he loved me, and it was up to me to make sure that love lasted.

And then, insidiously, he started to get angry again. I stayed calm, tried not to upset him, to agree with him. To say nothing. To walk away. I even tried to cry. There came a time when what he wanted was to burst out in anger, to empty the abscess.

My husband knew I was strong enough to protect the children from himself. That's why, when he got angry, the best thing I could do to calm him down was to go away. Alone with the kids, he would calm down, so afraid of his own violence. Deep down, he knew he was violent. This violence consumed him, so he directed it against the others, especially me, since I was the closest.

One day, when Pauline was just a baby, she cried a lot because she was hungry. I gave her a bottle. He was furious. He was hovering around me saying, "She's not going to bawl like that all day!" I calmly got up, put the baby in his arms, put the bottle down and said, "Well, you'll have to calm her down!

And off I went into the garden.

He found himself alone with the little girl and gave her a bottle, rocked her and she finally fell asleep. Then he came downstairs proudly, saying: "You see! I'm doing great!"

I was gnawing away at myself in my corner, but I knew it was better to do it this way. Before, I would have tried to calm him down, argued with him and he would have ended up screaming, shouting, hitting me with the little girl in his arms. Here, at least, he'd been forced to contain his anger and he was satisfied with that.

On another occasion, Jean jostled a vase as he ran through the living room. It fell to the floor and shattered. His father shouted from down the hall. I shouted louder than he did, motioning for Jean to go to his room. When his father arrived, I exclaimed: "Look what he's done! He's really unbearable, I gave him a good spanking and he's in his room..."

Jean, who had sensed the danger (but whom I hadn't touched), was crying in his corner. My husband set about gluing the vase back together, then said curtly: "There's no need to shout, it's your fault. If this vase wasn't accessible to children, it would still be in one piece...".

As a result, he didn't scold his son and the incident dissipated.

I was beginning to know how to stay out of trouble, and I gradually slipped into a form of permanent lying.

Evenings were often difficult and, above all, unpredictable. I never knew if I was going to be able to watch TV in peace or if he was going to come bellowing over to turn it off. So I invented internships, overtime, workshops. I'd put the kids to bed and leave again. I'd go to the movies, or see my brother. J.-P. is the only one of my three brothers who was really aware of the situation. Because he'd come on vacation with us and had the opportunity to see my husband's true face. He was my son's godfather and has always been a great support to me. At the time, my other brothers didn't live in Paris, and my sister, much younger than me, knew nothing about my life. At least, we never talked about it, and as I never confided in anyone, not even my parents, only J.-P., who witnessed certain scenes, could support and comfort me, even if I didn't tell him everything.

When I got home, my husband would be in bed and I'd slip quietly into bed. The children were asleep, safe, and I was at peace.

One day my brother said to me: "Can you believe it? You're lying when you're not doing anything wrong!"

I couldn't explain to him that I couldn't argue with my husband. I wasn't a meek and submissive woman, however, and I refused to let myself be beaten without retaliating. I was only willing to be submissive, to agree, when it was necessary to stop the crisis, when the children were around. But once they were alone, he pushed me to the limit. It was like an overflow of injustice suffocating me, of impotent rage. All I wanted was for him to disappear, to suffer and be destroyed forever.

After my rage, he finally had the upper hand and I was ashamed to behave like him. Especially as he said to me: "See the state you're in? You're crazy!"

I was not far from agreeing with him.

My son, on the other hand, guessed everything:

"Anyway, Mom, when Dad's around, your stomach hurts all the time! You say he's nice, but it's not even true..."

Stupidly, I replied:

- You know my darling daddy is tired..."

Until the day Jean's teacher called me in. My son was aggressive, hitting the younger children. On the way home, I tried to understand:

"Come on, Jean, why beat up on others? It's not right, you know...

- Well, I'm tired too... "

I understood my mistake and tried to explain to him that, tired or not, one shouldn't hit others, that it was inadmissible. The child knew very well how to retort:

"But Daddy does it and we don't tell him anything...

- Yes, but you see, when he was little, his mom should have explained it to him..."

I was obsessed with the idea that my children should have a stable childhood, and that to do this, they needed to be with both parents. I didn't realize that it didn't give them any balance to feel their mother constantly frightened, to be terrified of their father and subjected to an unbreathable family atmosphere.

One weekend, we spent a day in Honfleur with the kids. He was in a good mood until we stopped at a small restaurant.

He wanted tripe and decided to order it for everyone, even though he knew I didn't like it.

"But," I said, "not for children, of course, and I want fish.

- So for once, just once, you don't want to please me...

- But have some tripe if you like, on the contrary, but don't make us eat it!"

When the waitress came to take the order, he got up furiously and stormed out of the restaurant. She understood. She brought me steak frites and helped me feed the baby. I was on the verge of tears and couldn't swallow a thing. I tried to reassure Jean, who kept questioning me: "But where did Dad go? Did he take the car? How are we going to get home?"

After lunch, I took them to the bus station to return to Paris.

At one point, my son says to me, "Why do you always say 'Don't worry' to me?"

I didn't realize that I was so stressed that I kept repeating it over and over again.

Finally, he arrived by car, just as we were waiting for the bus.

I got the kids settled without saying a word and went upstairs. He grumbled through his teeth: "You haven't finished paying for this! You always have to ruin everything!"

Jean still remembers that trip to Honfleur.

As for me, I got into the habit of always leaving with papers, money and a credit card. I was so afraid he'd get us out of the car in a fit of anger.

When the kids weren't with us, things went better. He had less of a hold on me. I could resist him without fear. I answered him back, and when he insulted me, I said hurtful things. One day, I even threw my fist in his face and knocked out two of his teeth, in return for a slap he'd given me. As he bled over the sink, I said to him: "What do you think? If I don't fight back, it's only because of the children, poor thing, I'm stronger than you, I'd be able to kill you!"

I saw fear in his eyes, and a mixture of respect. It horrified me.

I'd just realized that if I wanted to get out of this, I had to act like him. Establish a balance of power and get the upper hand.

But I didn't want that relationship.

CHAPTER 5

I absolutely didn't want to fall into this trap. What would the kids think if we ended up fighting? What kind of example would we be setting for them? They'd end up like their father, living in this violence, or like me, a coward and a moron of misfortune... No, I didn't want that life for them.

I tried to put some distance between us.

As he had insomnia, I told him I'd be sleeping in the dining room from now on, so as not to disturb him. Obviously, he didn't like that. One night, I woke up, suffocating. Sitting on the edge of my bed, with an evil look in his eye, he was clutching my throat. I stood up, pushing him away.

"You were scared huh?"

He left the room. I was stunned. The next day, I bought a bolt and locked myself up to sleep. He almost kicked the door in.

He repaired it the next day. And he left me alone at night.

For a while, he got used to this distance. I'd get up before him in the morning, get the kids ready and we'd leave together. I'd leave the two older ones at school and the little one at nursery school, then go to work. In the evenings, he was often away, so I could look after the children in peace. He usually came home just as I was putting them to bed, and all I had to do was cook dinner.

Every other evening, I'd leave him to go to my so-called workshops or seminars. Focused on himself, as long as I told him it was for my work and that I wasn't amused by going out again, he'd leave me alone. "Why not tell the truth?" my friends would advise me. But the truth was, I avoided spending time with him for fear of a crisis. It was impossible to explain. Simply saying: "I'm going to the movies" would have been unacceptable to him. It meant granting me a space of freedom, a moment of pleasure, and the very idea was unbearable for him. On the contrary, if I looked tired, sighed and said "My God, I'm on call", or "I should never have signed up for that evening course"... he'd immediately urge me to go. He had to go against me, force me to force my nature; he couldn't help it, he called it "going forward".

"If it wasn't for me, my poor girl, you'd be sitting there like a stump, thank goodness I'm pushing you forward..."

He couldn't stand the fact that I was ill either: "Come on, get a move on, what's the point of staying in bed? You won't get better any faster... And in the meantime, I'm stuck with the kids!"

He was terrified of illness, both for himself and for those close to him. He dreaded dying at 37°2, and as for me, at the slightest touch of the flu, he feared above all that I would no longer be able to cope with a daily routine that would soon overtake him.

Once again out of work, he sailed from depression to uncontrolled euphoria. He could spend entire days smoking a pipe on the sofa without loosening his teeth, or, on the contrary, get up at six o'clock, get dressed singing at the top of his voice and leave all day, I wasn't sure where. He certainly didn't either. He'd visit friends and acquaintances, have coffee with them and talk about the misfortune that had befallen him. He'd come home, often annoyed and disappointed, and I'd pray that he'd find another job. I prayed that he would accept whatever was offered.

Eventually, he found it. I was relieved. He had negotiated one-off assignments. He would spend a month or two in the provinces.

I'd talk to the kids about him, he'd phone them, I'd phone him too, he'd say he missed me, I almost believed it. When he was away, our telephone conversations were always tender, and I began to believe again in the possibility of family life.

Then he'd come back, and after a couple of days I'd realize that I was trying terribly hard to keep the peace at home. He was less violent, but still verbally hurtful. Whenever I talked about my work, he would again belittle me: "What do you think, you're not a journalist, you write for an institutional rag!" Or again: "Well, your job's all very well, but you barely earn enough to keep the house running, I don't know how you manage... What would you do without me, eh?"

I'd stopped bringing work home because he was looking for mistakes in my articles. I think deep down, he was jealous. I had a job I loved, responsibilities, a circle of friends and even though he wanted to cut me off from the world, he couldn't really do it.

I compartmentalized my life. Nobody knew my husband, I never went anywhere with him, not even to my work. I always said he was out of town. I didn't talk about him much, but I didn't talk badly about him. I didn't want anyone to guess what I was going through, because I would have felt diminished, put down, too far from the image of the strong, cheerful woman I wanted to portray.

Because that's how people around me saw me, as someone who talked a lot, who had character, who knew how to express herself and say things. Who would have thought that, at home, I'd become someone else, a frightened victim, always on the alert, quick to throw up my hands to protect myself, evaluating a thousand strategies to keep a little serenity in this home I was imposing on my children? No, it was so inconceivable, I couldn't explain to myself why I put up with this life, so I preferred to hide it carefully.

I'd go on vacation to my parents' place in the South-West of France, without him. Little by little, the children became my world and he no longer counted. On several occasions, my son said to me: "Why don't we go away when he's not here? Why don't we do that, Mom?"

We also visited my husband's mother in Normandy, but there, everything was a pretext for conflict. He encouraged the children to make fun of her, and I watched in rage as this old lady I loved so much was humiliated.

In the end, I told him I'd go there alone; if he wanted to see his mother, he'd go his own way. He didn't object, convinced that I'd change my mind. But I never went back to my mother-in-law's with him for the next five years. Sometimes, he took his son with him. One day, Jean confided in me with all the lucidity of an 8-year-old: "You know, Dad's mean to Grandma, and I like Grandma, but he says he loves her, even though it's not true, otherwise why does he break her things?"

That day, I understood that I shouldn't excuse their father's behavior. That when he got angry and broke everything in the house, I had to tell them it was unacceptable behavior.

But I was afraid of shattering my father's image. I even found it hard to admit to myself that I didn't love him anymore. So much so that later, when the children would ask me: "But don't you love him any more, Dad?", I'd hear myself reply: "Of course I love him, but not like before...".

Anything! I was afraid that by admitting I didn't love their father any more, I was taking away a part of their love, something they were entitled to. I was afraid of breaking up the parental couple and hurting them. It took me years to understand that our relationship was harmful to them. I often hear people say to me: "Why didn't you leave earlier if it was really hell?"

Explaining that hell had become everyday life, but that it was sometimes disguised as paradise. That there were good moments when I caught myself hoping. That doubt and guilt made me believe that I was responsible for the situation and that I had the power and the duty to make things right. I could see that the children loved their father despite his temper (I think they still do to this day, in a way) and I didn't realize that they were conditioned, that they too, modelling their attitude on mine, were careful not to upset him, not to annoy him, that they ran off to their rooms at the slightest suspicious noise!

One day he bought pigeon-shooting equipment for his son. He dreamed about it, and the two of them had fun all afternoon. Jean would say to me, "When Dad bought me pigeon shooting, it was the happiest day of my life!" And I thought, "Do I have the right to deprive them of these moments?"

Yet insidiously, as the children grew older, I could see that they were looking at us in a way that spoke volumes about their understanding of the situation.

He ended up taking it out on them. First Jean, because he was the eldest.

He'd reprimand him for the slightest thing: on the pretext of checking his homework, he'd get angry and tear up his notebooks. I used to spend my evenings copying everything!

He scolded him off-line. In the morning, Jean would spill his bowl, his father would clean it up, and in the evening, as the boy came home from school, he would bark at him and slap him! Obviously, our son couldn't remember the morning's incident and was terrified. I tried to reason with his father:

"But there's no point in what you're doing, he needs to be scolded right away or not at all!

- Of course, with you you must never say anything," he replied, "children can destroy everything!"

He was locked into a logic of his own, circling like a fish in a barrel, and his anger was growing. It was as if it didn't always spring from an impulse, but ripened throughout the day, magnifying events like a snowball. If I hadn't said goodbye in the morning, he might greet me with a slap in the evening; if Jean had put the wrong cork in the toothpaste, he might calmly put it back in front of him and then put it in front of his plate at dinner, the prelude to a conflict that the child didn't always understand.

I came home as late as possible with the children after school, for baths and dinner. As my husband often went out in the late afternoon, I limited the time he could take it out on them. Similarly, on Saturdays, they all had activities and I also took them to the media library; on Sundays, we went to the swimming pool in the morning and to the public garden in the afternoon. I could never, never sit still with them at home when he was around. The drama was potential, and the crisis was brewing behind every one of his appearances.

On vacation, after two days he'd had enough. He'd disappear, screaming, with the car. But I still preferred that, running errands on foot with Dina in the stroller and bags at arm's length, to feeling him there, on the lookout, trying to figure out how to lash out, under what pretext to insult me.

Especially since, if he couldn't find a valid reason, he'd go and dismantle his car and then spend the afternoon complaining while fixing it. When it was the car, by the way, it was the lesser evil. One Saturday, he dismantled the washing machine, blew all the fuses and slammed the door. I spent the whole weekend in the dark, waiting for the repairman to arrive on Monday!

Sunday mornings were off to a good start. Breakfast together in a cheerful atmosphere. And then, as we passed in the hallway, he noticed that the chandelier in the entrance hall was dusty. By the time I went upstairs to dress the children, he'd got out the stepladder and dismantled the chandelier: "You'll see, I'm going to clean it all up...". Needless to say, the timing was bad, as we had to go for a walk. Still, I went out alone with the kids. When I came back, all the pieces of the chandelier were scattered and I was in a bad mood.

"Are you coming for lunch?

- Do you think that's all I've got to do?" he'd reply snappishly.

By the end of the day, at best the chandelier was gone, relegated to a corner and dismantled, and he'd sulk. At worst, he'd scream that it was all my fault, that I was incapable of running a house, that I was ruining his Sunday...

If things hadn't been so dreadful, they might have been funny to tell... Besides, my son quickly understood the situation and summed it up like this: "Dad, when everything's going well, decides to go and look at the car's engine... Then you're sure the day's ruined, because he's going to take it all apart and break it..."

One evening, on vacation, the children were playing on the terrace after their bath. I forbade them to roll around in the sand when they were in their pyjamas. But Pauline, seeing her father in the distance, ran towards him in her slippers. Jean shouted, "Mommy, Pauline's going in the sand!"

Their father arrived, said hello and I sent them off to brush their teeth.

Suddenly, a heavy step came up the stairs. I heard shouting and Jean screamed in fear. I rushed up. The boy was pale. His father had slapped him and was shaking him like crazy, shouting:

"You filthy cockroach! That'll teach you to fetch!"

I stepped in and took Jean in my arms, to calm him down.

- You're crazy! What are you talking about?

- I'm going to teach her to fetch when her sister goes in the sand..."

His eyes were bloodshot. I was pitted against him. He saw that I was angry and left abruptly.

For years, Jean was afraid of shouting and conflict. When he saw people in the street talking a bit heatedly, he'd move closer to me, trembling. He'd say to me: "I don't like it when we 'argue'...". He would also confide in me, "Daddy, he scares me!"

I began to think seriously that I had to leave him. But I was paralyzed. My brain was working at full speed, I was constantly adapting to conflict, surreal situations, mood swings; but I was blocked in my actions, unable to act, to take my children and leave. Everyday life was so difficult, I had my nose to the grindstone and not enough energy to work out any kind of escape strategy. I was so oppressed, so tense all the time. Every quiet moment, every day that was a little serene, gave me a chance to breathe. It was like a momentum I could use to get through the next few days. My whole body was hardened by constant attention, by a preoccupation with avoiding conflict that prevented me from even seeing the weather.

And yet the scenes continued to multiply, reaching heights that, little by little, pushed me over the edge.

One evening, he dragged Jean into the toilet, to put his nose in the urine he'd dropped next to the bowl. Jean cried and resisted. His father shook him and slammed the child's temple against the paper dispenser. He passed right by the eye: the wound was deep.

Furious, I threw myself at my husband and hit him like crazy. He protected himself but I was unleashed, I felt I could have killed him. I kept saying to myself: "Stop, stop, stop, you're going to do something terrible. When I finally calmed down, his jaw was completely swollen. I left him there and said, "Look at me now, if you ever raise your hand to one of the children again, I'll kill you, is that clear?"

I was ashamed of myself, ashamed of the violence he had the power to provoke, ashamed of the example I was setting for my children.

But at least that night he left me alone. I thought I'd taught him a lesson, made him understand something.

It got worse. In front of the children he would get all sweet and say: "Look at poor Mom, she's a little crazy, isn't she? She's not being nice to Dad...".

I understood his manipulation, I tried to be indifferent to it, but I feared it would confuse their little heads. Dina whined all the time, Pauline sometimes stared at me reproachfully with her strange clear eyes, and Jean shut herself away in her own world. Pauline, now grown up, once told me: "You know, Mum, when I was little, I thought you weren't very nice to Dad. I remember he'd give you presents and flowers and you'd never say thank you...".

She was too young at the time to remember that before she gave me the gifts in question, there had been the phase of destroying my things, insulting me and hitting me, often while they were in bed. The next day, he was charming, while everyone, starting with the children, found me morose and, to put it bluntly, not very likeable... Some in my own family still judge him to be a very pleasant man, but they only saw one side of his personality. Explaining things was beyond my powers. All the energy I could muster, I decided to reserve for running away.

One evening I told him we'd better separate. It was the first time I'd taken the initiative to talk about it; as for him, he often brandished the threat of divorce, without thinking for a second that I might have accepted... He shrugged: "Anyway, do you think you'll be able to get by without me with three children to support? Because if you leave, I won't give you anything, I'll go on unemployment and you'll have nothing... You know very well that I can live without working. I'll make myself insolvent. Try, try, my poor girl!

I didn't care. Material problems didn't scare me. Less frightening than my current existence. Besides, I had a job and a family, and I knew I'd have help. And above all, I realize today, I was young: at 32, you still have the courage to take charge of your life, and perhaps a certain recklessness. The women I met who didn't leave were often older, and their fears are greater. You feel more vulnerable as you get older.

When he felt he'd pushed me too far and that I was capable of leaving, he'd change tactics and start whining: "If you leave, I'll shoot myself in the head. (He didn't have a gun, but okay.) My life is you, and the kids... I mean, you know I love you..."

If he loved us, it was in a pathological way. For he was incapable of true love. He didn't like himself, and he'd ended up hating the very thing about me that he'd liked at first sight. My joie de vivre, my zest for life, my positive side. From then on, whenever he saw me laughing or smiling with the kids, he'd find a way to create drama. He'd look for any excuse to make me feel bad, and of course, children were the perfect tool for him... So I withdrew into myself, taking care never to be too cheerful in his presence, never to look happy, knowing that the reason for this fleeting happiness would inevitably be trampled underfoot.

So, one Christmas Eve, I had decorated the tree and, with the children in bed, I had put all the presents in their little slippers. I couldn't stand still, so I went looking for him to show him my work. Seeing the evil look on his face, I turned off the joy in my eyes, but a split second too late.

He began by grumbling, "That natural tree... You know I'm allergic... And then those presents... Ah that's just like you, all that matters is the kids! I bet dinner's not ready yet?"

And, of course, the meal wasn't ready.

Furiously, he kicked the presents, grabbed the tree and, before I could intervene, opened the window and threw it onto the sidewalk.

I was crying my eyes out when I went down to the street to pick up the decrepit tree as best I could. Really, I couldn't take it anymore.

I put the tree back as best I could and said, "I'm off to bed, so you can explain to the kids tomorrow why there's all this mess...".

I locked myself in the bedroom, letting him come and go in the living room. Later, he came scratching at my door, but I pretended to be asleep.

I finally fell into a nightmare-filled sleep until morning.

The children's cries of joy woke me up. I went into the living room. The tree was up, looking magnificent, presents piled high in the stockings. On the table, breakfast was served with a bouquet of roses. When he saw me, he stood up and exclaimed: "Ah, there's Mom! Did you sleep well, darling? Come and open the presents quickly!"

I remained a little stiff. I still had sobs in my throat, but the children were overjoyed, jumping up and down amidst their presents. So I made an effort to look relaxed.

Later, my in-laws came for lunch and my husband rivalled them in gaiety, getting up to serve ("Stay seated, darling..."), playing with the overexcited children running around the living room ("Leave them alone, it's Christmas...").

My sister-in-law, a little more refined than the others, took me aside as she left:

"How are you? Are you transparent, are you in trouble?

I felt like bursting into tears, but I restrained myself:

- No, no, just a little tired...

And my mother-in-law exclaimed:

- Anyway, you're lucky to have such a nice husband, he's a great help! He's tidying up..."

Looking back, I understand the people who testified against me at the time of the divorce, repeating what my husband told them, that I was ill, fragile, even a little disturbed. They didn't see the kind father throwing the Christmas tree out of the window, they didn't see the exemplary husband hitting me with a chair because I dared to protest, they didn't hear the cries of a little 9-year-old boy, locked in his room amidst his uselessly torn notebooks.

I kept thinking that one day things might change.

Chapter 6

After a while, after he'd stopped his therapy and medication, I think he finally understood that we couldn't live together anymore. He could see that I was rebelling. What's more, the children were growing up and I sensed, and I'm sure he did too, that they weren't happy between us.

But every time I mentioned the possibility of separation, he'd find himself on a three-month mission at the end of the world. Since Dina's birth, he had hardly ever lived with us. He blamed me for the state of our relationship. Unable to question himself, he preferred to think that everything was my fault. And when he sensed that I was becoming too rebellious, when he saw that he'd crossed the line, he'd back-pedal and we'd have a moment of calm.

One of his few friends asked him one day:

"Don't you think your wife will go away one day?

And he laughed, not knowing that I could hear him:

- Are you kidding? I'm always catching up, it's like a fish at the end of the line..."

For my part, I ran into a childhood friend I hadn't seen for a long time, in a public garden near our house where I often took the children. She admired the little ones, and we talked about our shared youth. Suddenly she asked me: "What's happened to you? Have you become extinct, you who were so full of life?"

And instead of telling the truth, of recounting the hell of my daily life, I blamed this fatigue on my work, the children, the loss of my babies...

Why didn't I talk to anyone for so many years, not my friends, not even my family?

I think I was ashamed to put up with all that violence, and ashamed to admit that I hadn't been able to save our marriage. I also realized that my husband's attitude was inexplicable. I was afraid of not being believed, especially by those who saw him from time to time and with whom he showed his best side.

On one occasion, my mother must have understood that I was in a bad way, because she hugged me and said, "Ah! Sometimes life is difficult, isn't it?"

I didn't seize the opportunity. In fact, I wouldn't have known where to start. And when I tried to make sense of it, I was horrified to realize that things had started badly, which only added to my guilt. "Come on," I convinced myself, "if you're still here after all these years, it must be that things aren't so bad!" I didn't know how to justify myself or my decisions, whatever they were. Besides, my parents didn't dislike him at first - on the contrary. A pleasant, well-educated man from a good background, with a respectable job. When the mask fell off, it took me a while to believe it myself. I was desperate to find the man who had seduced me, who was so interesting, so thoughtful, who everyone liked. How could I explain to everyone what I had become?

Only my brother J.-P. and a friend understood me. The latter had lived through a similar story. And I didn't even need to explain the situation to her. She understood what I didn't say, never asked me any questions, and was immensely supportive.

I often went to her house to recharge my batteries. She'd reassure me: "No, you're not crazy at all, it's normal that it's hard, you're going through difficult things..." She'd add: "You know, when you've lived like I have with a temperamental person, you can spot them...". She added: "You know, when you've lived with a temperamental person like I have, you can spot them..."

Which is true. Today, I can immediately sense when a man is potentially violent. I can sense this disposition from a distance, and sometimes I stiffen up when faced with men who have done nothing to me, but in whom I detect violence. It's like a sixth sense. Like a dog used to sniffing out drugs, I can decipher temperamental behavior, and the masks come off as soon as I'm in the presence of an unstable, potentially aggressive man.

I was exhausted, overwhelmed, but I had my job, and there I was active and successful. This job saved my life. Eight hours a day, I was doing something else and pushing problems to the back of my mind.

And then there were the children, I looked after them a lot and spent all my free time with them. I organized outings and parties, and as often as possible, I tried to exclude their father. Didn't he like the sea? I'd take them to Deauville. He hated movies? I had tickets for the Grand Rex. Didn't like my parents? Too bad, but I took the kids to them on vacation. He reproached me, we didn't do anything together anymore, we lived next door to each other and he certainly suffered from it.

But I understood that indifference was a weapon against him. I didn't answer him, I let him bully me, and when I felt he was on his last legs, I left. I often sought refuge at our neighbor Sylvie's house. I'd stay with her for an hour, then invite her home.

She was my safeguard. He feared her a little, but she was a big, strong woman, a nurse who didn't hesitate to put him in his place. And in front of her, he tried to be charming even when he was boiling. When I'd come in and shout playfully, "Sylvie's come for tea", he'd have to be just about calm.

This neighbor was the first to understand the situation. She had witnessed his violence towards the children, and if she tried to remain neutral, it was because she knew that by doing so she could help us.

I think she was one of the few people not afraid of him. At the time of the divorce, my mother-in-law, who owned the building, went round the neighbors, accompanied by her son, ordering them to testify against me or face eviction. The building was still under the 1948 law, with very low rents, and the tenants feared they would have to leave if the owners carried out any work that would legally allow them to raise the rent. Only two people didn't testify against me. Sylvie and the janitor, a brave and courageous Portuguese woman, who threw them out of her dressing room, shouting: "Isn't that a pity? Such a sweet, kind lady, I'll never, ever write anything against her..."

She even went up to see the old lady on the second floor to forbid her to sign anything: "Otherwise I won't do your housework anymore... It's shameful, you know, I know what he's like, I can see him, I can hear him!..."

People didn't risk much though, the law protected them. But everyone looked out for their own interests, and perhaps they were all convinced that I was hysterical, deranged...

One of the neighbors explained that my children were making noise on the stairs, the other that I cried all the time (a sign of mental problems, of course), the third that "my" sons (although I only have one) had caused a water leak by making the bathtub overflow (which was true, by the way, but didn't make me a bad mother).

I didn't want to get involved in this petty, gratuitous game of accusations, and I didn't have anyone around me to do it. All I could do was ask those close to me for written evidence that I was a normal person, a good mother, testimonials "for" me but not "against" him.

What do you want," I had to tell my lawyer, "he's never laid a hand on me in public, so I can't make up testimony...

And he, with a shrug:

- You're very scrupulous. You know, in this kind of fight, 99% of what's written is wrong..."

I think I still didn't dare involve people in our sordid life. I didn't think he'd burden me so much either. I told myself that deep down, he must have known that it was over between us, that the situation wasn't viable.

I didn't understand that by leaving him, I was taking away his toy, his whipping boy. He couldn't tolerate it, and no amount of reasoning would help. In his mind, nothing and nobody could stand in the way of his desire, his pleasure, his immediate enjoyment.

I knew the words that hurt him, I knew his flaws, I could hurt him too. Freed from the presence of the children, I took pleasure in challenging him, in resisting him. I'd phone for hours when he was around, lock myself in my office, make nothing to eat, let him cook dinner only to tell him I wasn't hungry. In a word, I took revenge by being obnoxious.

But it wasn't what I wanted. Neither for me nor for the children. When I see photos of myself from that time, I'm ugly, white, sad.

A friend once asked me:

"But you've never cheated on him?

- No..."

I didn't have the strength to meet anyone and, in any case, those ten years with him had permanently shaken my confidence in men in general. I just longed for solitude and serenity.

As this friend said to me, after her long and bitter divorce: "If someone had asked me to stay a nun all my life, I would have signed...".

Because we no longer believe in anything, in happiness, we're devastated.

Some people also said to me: "It took a lot of courage for you to leave with three children...".

It's not courage. When you're on the edge of a precipice with flames behind you, you jump, you have no choice. There's no courage, it's the only way out.

True courage is daring to understand this in time.

My husband sensed that I couldn't stand this life any longer, and wisely took on two more missions. He was on the lookout, sensing that the limit had been reached, and he in turn tried to fix the situation. Not out of love, no, out of manipulation, he was devising stratagems to prevent me from escaping his grasp. The idea was simply unbearable for him. But he couldn't look me in the eye and say: "I love you, I want to save our relationship, tell me how", language that would undoubtedly have touched me. No, he said: "You've no right to leave me, I've trusted you, if you leave you'll be betraying me...".

These words troubled me, but the love had finally gone. As the sea withdraws and leaves the wet sand full of shells and seaweed, its violence had settled inside me like alluvium, and I felt an energy rising up to replace my feelings.

I first contacted a lawyer. I spoke to him in an uncertain voice, not knowing what to do or how to explain things. I was confused, afraid that my husband would suddenly burst into the apartment. I wasn't sure what to do.

The lawyer replied very simply: "I don't think you're ready yet... When your husband comes home, try to talk it over with him and when you've decided to separate, don't hesitate to call me back."

I was worried about so many things: material security, my small salary, the house he would keep (because, as he had told me often enough, I was staying with him), my friends and the pain I would cause my family, who would worry...

Around the same time, my husband began to have health problems. He was neglecting his medication and taking uncontrolled doses of antidepressants and Lexomil. One day, the housekeeper found him suffocating in the living room. Distraught, she called the doctor: angioedema. He prescribed treatment and advised me to keep an emergency kit on hand just in case.

One night, I woke up to an unusual noise coming from the living room. He often got up, but now I heard a kind of moaning. Immediately, I thought: "That's it, he's having an attack again, an edema...". I jumped out of bed, my first move being to run and get the kit to give him an injection of anti-histamine, as the doctor had shown me.

And then suddenly, I sat back down. What if I did nothing? I stood there in silence, listening to his jerky breathing. Images flashed through my mind. I'd found my husband dead in the early hours of the morning, I was free, I could even mourn him.

Then, all of a sudden, I felt ashamed of myself and rushed off.

He was suffocating in the armchair, so I grabbed the kit and slipped a tablet under his tongue while I prepared the injection.

After a few minutes, he was breathing easier.

I called the doctor, all the same, who congratulated me: "You've done very well," he said, "he could have stayed there, especially as it's the second time."

He whimpered. He was scared and wanted me to stay with him that night. I went up to his room and lay down beside him. He fell asleep and I was left with my guilt. To think I was ready to let him die, to commit a crime! I didn't know myself to be so cruel. If I refused to be a victimized and humiliated woman, I also didn't want to become the cantankerous shrew that was growing inside me. My mind was made up, I would leave him. I wasn't going to buy my peace with his death and give my children a criminal mother.

I don't know if he realized I'd taken so long to come. He thanked me the next day and even bought me a piece of jewelry, a small gold ring (which he was to confiscate rather quickly, by the way!).

But how many times did the idea of his accidental death cross my mind? I'd imagine coming home from work in the evening, or finding him in bed in the morning, and I'd even imagine how sorry I was! Because I knew that at that moment, I'd get sympathy, help, that people would support me.

At the time, leaving my husband meant doing myself a disservice and staying in a difficult situation. No one would understand if I left a man who was so attached to his family, who went to the ends of the earth to ensure our well-being, with whom I'd had three children, to live alone in precariousness... My mother, to whom I made a few allusions, probably understood, but not completely, since I never went into detail. My best friend told me to question my feelings. It seemed to him that I still loved the father of my children, and besides, that's how it had always been, so why not put up with it all of a sudden?

Really, why? What are the reasons that lead a woman to live through ten years of hell, believing that paradise will eventually exist, and who overnight no longer wants to live through this hell? What's the limit of what's bearable?

Mine was reached the day I realized that my children were suffering the full brunt of this violence, and that things weren't going to get any easier. Jean was growing up, and who knows? maybe one day he too would fight with his father?

As my eldest daughter was to say to me later, "As far as I'm concerned, you saved us from Daddy!"

I'd always believed that a couple who stayed together for their children was better than parents who were apart. That as long as the children were there, we should stay together. But the examples around me at the time gradually showed me otherwise, and helped me to take that decisive step.

A friend of mine who, like me, had three children, arrived at the park one day in a state of confusion: "My parents are getting divorced...".

She was on the verge of tears, full of anger and incomprehension. She told me:

"They explained to us that they stayed together because of us kids. My last brother's married and now they're splitting up, how crazy is that?"

I tried to understand his confusion:

- Yes, of course, but in a way, you can be grateful to them, because deep down, they've kept you safe, and if you didn't suspect it, it's because they've managed to give you a harmonious childhood in spite of everything...

She interrupted me furiously:

- But don't you understand? That's just it, they've deceived us, betrayed us... All these values on which I've based my own life, it's all a fake, a wind, a vast deception..."

I told myself that I would have acted the same way if I'd had a calmer, more understanding husband. That I would have been willing to sacrifice part of my life to ensure a certain financial and emotional stability for my children. But, in the face of my friend's confusion, I suddenly realized how important the truth was, and how important it was to speak the truth to the children.

Making them believe in a love that no longer exists, in a couple that no longer even sleeps together, what will that lead them to later? How will they know if what they're experiencing is really happiness if they've never met it?

I had another friend who lived quietly with a husband and two little girls. He cheated on her, and she was often red-eyed, but she stayed: "As long as he comes back to us, it's because we're more important to him, and I'd rather be unhappy with him than without him... That's how it is...". Yet her daughters suffered to see their mother unhappy.

What harm are we doing to our children by accepting the unacceptable?

For mine, the damage was already done.

Their daily lives were woven of violence, terrorizing screams and anguishing whispers. From unspoken words (we're leaving for school early, Dad's having a fit) to lies (I've got a great idea, instead of going home we'll go to McDonald's... Dad's here earlier than planned), my children, especially Jean, were quick to read my eyes and know when it was time to shut up or leave the room.

I, who loved them so much, had filled their dreams with frightful nightmares, bathing their reality in a nervous tension that changed according to their father's moods.

I'd got it all wrong.

But it wasn't too late, I'd stayed for them, now I was going to leave for them.

Chapter 7

In May 1991, I was promoted to head of reporting at my newspaper's editorial office. I was delighted, because I was supervising young aspiring journalists who had come from journalism schools to do their military service.

I was well organized, the children were all at school, a young girl looked after them in the evenings and took them to their various activities on Wednesdays.

My husband was in a bad mood because, once again, he didn't have a job. He was a good professional, but his temperament prevented any constructive career. He'd been back from the provinces for two months and was going in circles.

He was so annoyed with the children that I asked the girl to keep them in the garden as long as possible, in fact until I arrived...

He'd go through my things, my papers, thinking I was hiding something, or someone, from him. It's true that I told him as little as possible about who I was with and what I was doing. All my energy was focused on the children I had to protect and on my job, in which I felt valued.

One day my son scolded me and said, "First of all, you're useless, you don't know how to do anything, your job is shit!"

In his mouth, his father's words! It made me so uncomfortable that I couldn't even pick him up again. Things weren't going very well for him at school, and the dreaded academic failure was looming. School was a chore on top of the ordeal he was going through at home.

On the contrary, for the girls, it was an escape, a place of serenity where they could deposit the overflow of anxieties they were experiencing at home.

Once, just once, when she was in CE1, Pauline cried. Their father had screamed in the morning and thrown my things down the stairs. Outside the school gate, she burst into tears. I crouched down and wiped her little face: "My darling, don't cry, you're going to have a good day and tonight everything will be fine... You have to go to school, you know..."

She calmed down. At the end of the day, she told me that she had cried a little in class and that the teacher had asked her why:

"I told him I was tired of Daddy yelling all the time and that I was scared....

- And what did she say?

- Well, she said not to worry about it, that it was grown-up stuff and that I shouldn't worry about it... And she gave me a piece of candy..."

This teacher rose in my esteem and, at the same time, I felt mortified. She must have thought I was leading a strange life for my daughter!

One evening, at last, I stopped thinking and took action. He came home just as I was putting the kids to bed, and announced in a jovial tone: "Come on! Let's go to the restaurant, I've got a surprise!"

I was tired. His days started at 3 p.m., and we were always living out of sync. I didn't feel like going out, and who could I entrust the children to? As usual, my tone was immediately upbeat: "Voilà! Never happy! As soon as I suggest something out of the ordinary, it's a no! My God, you've become such a homebody! What about the kids? But they can stay on their own, we're going next door..."

Once again, I decided not to upset him. I went to see Jean, who wasn't asleep:

"My darling, we're going to the diner, not far, if you have any worries, you go down to the babysitter's, O.K.?

- Yes, yes," he replied, looking serious and responsible (too responsible for his 9 years), "don't worry Mom, there won't be any problem..."

I combed my hair and ran down the stairs. He stood in front of the door, frozen like the statue of the Commander.

In the street, the June evening was warm and the boulevard smelled of acacias and garden honeysuckle. It was a beautiful evening, a time for lovers. And I was dragging my feet behind my husband, who was taking me out for couscous without even asking me if I liked it...

As soon as he was seated, he smiled at me and took my hand above the table. I smiled back. I was in a knot, but I tried to relax: for once he was all right, I didn't want to spoil it with my anxieties.

He ordered a royal couscous, served me wine and announced:

"I've just been offered a job in Martinique, all expenses paid, with my family, including moving, for a minimum of three years. I've accepted, you think? It'll be great for us, a new start," he tells me tenderly.

- What about my job?

- Your job? (He swept the problem aside with a gesture.) But with what I'm going to earn, you have time to find another one, my darling...

I couldn't breathe, my plate was untouched and I froze in place.

- Well?" he asked.

He was half worried and half annoyed. I think he seriously thought I was going to be delighted. He was too egocentric to think for a second about the upheavals in my life and those of the children. It was good for him, that's all that mattered. He ate with pleasure, poured himself wine, he was happy, relaxed and I thought: what the hell, he's completely off his rocker!

Suddenly, I heard myself utter these astonishing words. As if another person were speaking through my voice:

"Listen... It's a great idea, but you're going to go alone... I'm not going... There's no way.

He put on the stubborn expression of a spoiled child:

- What I want is for us to leave together, that's all.

I looked at him for a moment and resumed:

- You can do exactly as you like, but I'm going to leave you anyway. So it might be a good idea for you to take this job, it might help you..."

I was expecting an outburst of violence, or a scornful, hostile reproach. But I think he understood instantly that my mind was made up. He had certainly read my determination in my eyes: he knew me well enough to know that it was irrevocable. He didn't get angry, just gave me a pained glance, grabbed his jacket and left the restaurant.

Something unraveled in my chest. I ate with good appetite, I even finished my glass!

I was free and no longer afraid.

When I went back up to the apartment, he wasn't there.

I went to the children's room. Their steady breathing gave me confidence.

At the foot of their beds, I made a promise: "We're going to make it, that's for sure, life's going to be good now!"

He came home around five in the morning and threw himself on my bed, crying. He kept repeating:

"I love you, I don't want to lose you, I understand my mistakes, I'll change, I promise.

- You see," I said, "you go away, you come back in the morning, and you don't wonder if the kids are alone?"

I felt very sorry for him, compassionate even. At that moment, I wished I could go back, tell him I loved him, that I was going to leave with him. But I couldn't anymore. It was over, I knew clearly that I was no longer in love and that our story was over. It was like a force, a great summer wind, like invisible hands leading me, at last, on my own road to happiness and serenity.

For the next few days, he cried all the time. The children didn't understand, he would tell them, "Mommy is mean to me," and Dina would push me with her little fists, "Mean Mommy!" Jean remained silent but looked at me incredulously, Pauline, with her usual confidence, seemed pleased.

I explained:

"Children, I'm going to leave Daddy, I don't love him anymore, we're going to live somewhere else, but you can see him whenever you like, of course...

- How soon? Right away?" asked Jean.

- It's going to take some time...

- What if Dad doesn't want to?

- Too bad, he'll have to...

- Well, he's not going to be happy..."

My little man was worried. I reassured him as best I could, assuring him that their father would come to see them in our new apartment. To my surprise, he exclaimed: "But Mom, no, you mustn't tell him. If you tell him where we're going, he'll kill us..."

What image did he already have of his father, what fear gripped him?

A few days later, my husband told me:

"Okay, look I'll take the job in Martinique, but promise me one thing... Stay here, in the apartment with the kids and think it over. If when I get back you haven't changed your mind, then we'll divorce, but please, take this time.

- But I've thought it all through, I won't change my mind, I've already seen a lawyer...

- Look, we've lived together for almost twelve years, you can give me a year to think things over before you scuttle the whole thing, can't you? What I'm asking is that you don't start any proceedings while I'm away..."

I promised. I was relieved that he'd made this decision, I told myself I'd have time to look around, to look for an apartment. So he signed his contract for one year, renewable twice. He was calm, telling me over and over again: "I trust you, don't I? You won't send the lawyers after me while I'm away?"

I explained the situation to my lawyer, telling him that, for the time being, I would postpone the divorce. But fortunately for me, I had already started proceedings a few weeks earlier, and my lawyer had sent a draft petition for divorce on accepted demand, which my husband immediately tore up. When, much later, he dared to declare to the judge that I had decided to leave him while he was far away, working to feed his family, I was able to prove that my intention to divorce had been well in advance of his departure.

Even then, he had a talent for rewriting history in his own way. During the fortnight before his departure, his family and a few friends took turns trying to make me understand how wrong I was, how wrong I was to make a man who adored me suffer.

My sister-in-law said to me one day: "But can you believe it, he's moving abroad to offer you and your children a better life, and you want to leave him?"

My mother-in-law added, "Well, you know he adores you."

And the friends in chorus: "Come on, you know he only lives for you and the kids!"

I tried to explain, to justify myself. But no one could understand, admit or hear that a smiling, intelligent, kind and loving man could turn into an odious, howling beast as soon as the door closed on the guests. Who could believe that he would sneak up beside me at night and pretend to strangle me? That I'd come home in the evening to find the house devastated, my papers torn up, the children's toys in the garbage?

It was too complicated to prove the facts. Apart from those very close to me, who understood immediately, either because they had witnessed it or because they knew me well enough, I once again walled myself up in a silence that did me no favors.

My husband still thought things could be fixed, that he could change my mind. But I had become someone else. My role as a victim, as a weak and ashamed woman, had horrified me from the moment I'd realized that this trip to Martinique was going to close a terrifying trap on our lives. I'd been living a hard life, but this was hell, and my instinct was to reject this exile with all my might. I had experienced Morocco. I'd been happy there, but I'd sensed that I was at his mercy, for the work, for the duration of the stay. And back then, we didn't have any children. Going overseas today meant giving up a rewarding professional life, being under his financial control, breaking with my family and friends, and leaving for a world that was threatening because it was precarious and indefinite.

My son was to say to me one day: "Dad, you mustn't be in his clutches, as long as you can escape, it's okay, he holds back, but when you're forced to stay close to him, it's terrible, it's the end…".

He knew that, having given him my word, I would do nothing against him while he was away. He thought he was preparing a tactic. But for my part, my decision was irrevocable. I took advantage of this time of solitude to recharge my batteries.

I had broken my shackles and realized that decisions belonged to me too.

I was adrift in my life and, all of a sudden, I was back at the oars.

CHAPTER 8

One Monday in June 1991, I accompanied my husband with a couple of friends, my husband's godfather and his wife, who were very kind, to Roissy airport. Without emotion, I watched him disappear. He was sick and sad. He was a sight to behold. But I felt detached, calm. I didn't dare to be happy yet. I convinced myself that he wouldn't come back and that I'd be at peace.

His godfather said to me in the car, as he was driving me back to Paris: "You know, his problem is that up until now (i.e. until he was 45), he's never been annoyed... Now you can't do as he pleases, it's unbearable for him...".

He told me about his childhood. The boarding school in Switzerland, his difficulties at school, which strangely reminded me of my son's, the car accident that took the life of his fiancée when they were 25... He had never been helped, never been listened to in his pain and torment. In those days, you had to fend for yourself, and he didn't know how.

He'd built himself up the wrong way and made me pay for my happy childhood, my cheerful character and, above all, my taste for life, which he couldn't admit because he was totally devoid of it. I had access to the joy of life and he was frustrated to the point of hatred.

His godfather told me that I had to support him, that he had become aware of the harm he was doing to me, that he didn't want to lose me, and that he was convinced he could change: "It's too late," I kept telling him, "I can't be his nurse anymore, the one who listens, reassures him, cares for him, I can't be his whipping boy, I can't do it anymore...".

I could see he was really hurting, but I also knew it was over for both of us. I didn't want to hurt him. I was never out for revenge. I just wanted peace. I just wanted peace.

Of course, everyone had something to say. He had beaten his drums in public, in front of his family, and was hiding behind his illness. He was making efforts to cope, even consulting a shrink, he had taken medication; I knew all this, but I also understood that it would always be like this. He couldn't change.

When someone close to him managed to make him realize that he'd done wrong by bullying me and terrorizing the children, he'd reply that it was my fault, that I'd pushed him to the limit, that the attempted divorce had finished him off and that only I could restore his serenity.

I'd agreed to play along, to suspend the proceedings, to stay in the apartment, to explain to the children that Dad had gone off to work. His family breathed, mine too, everyone thought things would settle down. Only I knew that the time for separation had come.

The summer vacations were magnificent, calm and sunny. I returned rested as never before. The children smiled, sang and invited friends. Pauline wanted a cat, and she got one, nicknamed Alsace, a black-and-white ball the kids went crazy for.

The new school year got off to a peaceful start. Jean had a young master, and he worked well.

I really felt better. I thought he'd understood and would stay away indefinitely, a way of controlling from a distance, avoiding the inevitable. I was naive.

On All Saints' Day, without warning, he returned for eight days. He was having a hard time, alone, exiled to the ends of the earth and, he added, he wanted to see if I'd "made any progress in my thinking". It was a terrible stay. He almost killed the little cat, on whom he threw the iron before locking her in the cupboard. My concierge, outraged, took the poor animal in, completely terrorized.

In the evenings, I'd take the kids home, look after them and go to sleep at my brother's place. I tried to avoid all contact, but arguments broke out all the same.

He blocked access to his account and decided not to pay me any more money. I didn't care, I could manage on my salary.

Until the day the tax form arrived. It was for twenty-five thousand francs! Obviously, I couldn't pay and he ignored my pleas. Then I remembered that long ago he had given me power of attorney over the Caisse d'Epargne. Which easily gave me the sum I needed to pay the taxes.

I was to discover on this occasion that he had almost a hundred thousand francs in stocks and bonds, and that rent from a building in Paris was paid into an account every month. I had lived with this man for over ten years, and I didn't even know how much money we had! I paid the day-to-day expenses out of my salary, my mother-in-law gave us the rent as a gift, and he paid the bills and made the big purchases, like the car and washing machine. Everything else was saved up and I knew nothing about it.

Months later, my friends would say to me: "But you should have taken the whole hundred thousand francs! You'd have been in the clear instead of struggling like you did!"

But at the time, I didn't care about the money; I just wanted to pay those taxes. I didn't even realize that, while he had power of attorney over my account, I didn't have access to anything. He'd only signed that power of attorney when his father died because he wasn't in a position to take the necessary steps. Fortunately for me!

I didn't want to rob him or take his money. I regretted it later. Because he would refuse to give me back my things and those of the children, he would plunder my Codévi and cut me off, leaving me to fend for myself with the children. When he accused me of selling things that belonged to him, I'd think to myself, "What a fool, that's what I should have done!"

He had never been generous - not a gift, not anything superfluous - but I lacked nothing. When he stopped paying the bills, it was a really difficult time. I managed to find a second job. I worked the evening switchboard at a private clinic. My neighbor and friend looked after the sleeping children, but only Jean knew about it.

Little by little, I felt alive again, able to face life and explain things in a calm, rational way.

I cried less often, felt less of the lump rising and falling in my throat. I looked around and it was spring.

I'd met someone called Patrick, a kind and tender young man who helped me get through it. I saw him from time to time and it was the first time in a long time that someone had been kind to me. Even if the relationship wasn't meant to last, it made it easier for me to get through this painful period.

And then one day, on the eve of Jean's communion, one of my husband's cousins called me in a panic: "Please don't say I warned you, but he's coming back, he's arriving in three days, he's mad as hell, he says he'll kill you rather than let you leave him... Please, take care of yourself..."

She was crying and completely panicked. He had called his godfather and she had overheard the conversation.

I asked my parents to take the children away after the communion ceremony. Easter vacation was eight days away, and they could miss school. This mass, which should have been a beautiful moment, was lived in anguish. I kept looking around, fearing to see him arrive: perhaps the cousin had got the date wrong?

I explained to the children that they would be going on vacation earlier than planned. They were delighted. I didn't tell them their father was coming home, I wanted them to have a quiet vacation. I knew their father wouldn't dare go to my parents' house.

I entrusted the cat and goldfish to my neighbor and packed a suitcase.

My lawyer warned me: "Don't leave before you've talked to him, otherwise you'll be in the wrong. Try to have a frank conversation and then go to your parents' or a friend's house."

I was hanging out the washing in the bathroom when I heard the front door. He slammed it shut and shouted:

"Are you there?"

I stepped into the hallway. He was already beside himself in the middle of the living room:

- You've moved the furniture around... and you're making a real mess when my back is turned!

He saw me and grabbed me by the shoulders, brutally.

- Where's my cane? My silver cane?

I disengaged myself and tried to speak calmly:

- But she's upstairs, in the study...

He leapt up the stairs and returned with the cane. Before I had time to duck, he'd broken it across my back. The blows rained down and I couldn't hear him anymore.

The doorbell rang.

The frightened neighbor across the street asked:

- What's going on?

I went into the kitchen and picked up the wall phone. Trembling, I called my brother's house. He was at work, and I only had time to whisper to my sister-in-law:

- Quick, tell J.-P. to come and get me...

My husband lunged at me, ripping the phone from its cradle. The wire was dangling on the floor, and he screamed as he grabbed my wrists.

In front of the dumbfounded neighbor, he explained:

- My wife is having a nervous breakdown, I'm trying to calm her down but it's difficult. Come on, darling, let's...

I was in tears, flushed, my face streaked with marks, trembling. He, very calm and affable, gently let go of my hand and stroked my cheek. The neighbor couldn't help but notice my involuntary sidestep. I took the opportunity to walk down the corridor. I grabbed my bag and went out, leaving the neighbor between us. I ran down the stairs. He shouted over the banister:

- If you leave, you can never come back, I warn you!

I was running down the sidewalk when I heard the horn honking. My brother was coming. I collapsed crying against him.

He calmed me down and said:

- Well, let's go back upstairs and get your things, and I'll come with you...

- No, no... I'm too scared...

He finally convinced me and we both went upstairs. I had the key and my brother opened the door because I was shaking so much. My husband saw him and came storming in:

- She stays outside, she's forbidden to stay here!

And, pointing to the snatched phone:

- Did you see what she did?

My brother was taller and more imposing than he was. My husband, on the other hand, had never been very brave. Hitting a woman or children, yes, but never going up against someone stronger than him!

My brother dismissed it with a wave of his hand and said:

- Get your things...

I rushed to my room to retrieve the suitcase I'd packed a few days earlier. I had my papers, some jewelry, a few clothes, that's all.

He shouted:

- You'll never set foot in here again...

- That's for sure," retorted my brother, "she'll never come here again!"

I was clutching my suitcase. My brother forced me to lodge a complaint, but the local police explained to me that I should have stayed at home, that having left the marital home, I was at fault... J.-P. interrupted him curtly:

- Yes, but she's alive!..."

I was thinking about the children. Not once in those final moments had my husband asked me where they were. He was walking in circles around the apartment, cataloguing everything.

His only fear was that something was missing. He was convinced I'd stolen it...

I heard from a friend that he went to the school the next day and questioned the principal. He had an affidavit drawn up claiming that I had "unschooled" the children, that I had made them take an extra eight days' vacation to prevent him from seeing them.

It was April 1992, and the war had begun in earnest.

He no longer begged me to come back with him, no longer said he was unhappy without me. He'd moved on to threats. He would wait for me outside my office and follow me to find out where I lived. He'd tell me he'd kill me, kill the children. Even though I knew his threats were empty, I couldn't help feeling scared.

I called my lawyer. He was on vacation. His associate, a young woman, after listening to me, said:

"Madam, you did the right thing by leaving and taking your children to safety. With your work stoppage for assault and battery, I'm going to ask for urgent measures so that you can be allowed to live separately...

- I'm told I'm at fault.

- So what? That's not the point, I'm here to defend you, don't worry..."

Perhaps because she was a woman, she understood right away that I couldn't go back home. She also understood the urgency of the situation for the children. Less than a month later, we were summoned to the Paris Court of First Instance for a conciliation hearing.

If my lawyer hadn't been on vacation, I wouldn't have had this replacement lawyer who really took charge of things. My lawyer made sure I didn't make any mistakes, that I wasn't in the wrong; her aim was to protect me, "the rest is my job", she kept telling me. I think she had a better grasp of the situation and, above all, of the seriousness of a possible act by my husband, who had become furious.

As he put it, "I've got nothing left to lose, if I kill you all I'll kill myself next." Even though I didn't really believe it, I felt the familiar fear invade me and sap my strength. Sheltered with a friend, the children in the country with my parents, I measured the temporary nature of the situation and feared more than anything that I would be forced to return to live with him.

In the meantime, I went to work and only talked to my closest colleague. I clung to my job. I wanted to remain as normal and natural as possible, too afraid that people would take the opportunity to shoot me in the back, a common practice when people feel weakened.

So I worked like crazy and listened to my lawyer's advice. I really prayed that on the day of the hearing, the judge would agree to separate residency. That day, and that day only, I'd get the kids back.

On May 7, 1992, we were both in the judge's chambers.

Chapter 9

My lawyer warned me: "This is the only time you'll really be able to talk to the judge and explain your story. You have to defend your steak, it's your only chance, after that, everything will happen without you..."

I remember standing on the bridge, looking out over the Seine not far from the Palais de Justice. Patrick was with me and my sister. I felt completely helpless. And then, suddenly, I exclaimed: "Well, I'm off" and planted them there, walking away towards the Palais. It was like jumping into the water.

It was time for the face-off.

The day before, I had come alone to scout the place. I knew exactly where the judge's chambers were. But today, the corridors seemed endless and all I could think of was that he'd get there before me, that he'd be waiting for me. But only my lawyer was waiting for me.

He appeared a few minutes later, preceded by his lawyer. He seemed very calm. He approached me to say hello, and I instinctively stepped back. He made a weary movement and shrugged his shoulders, as if to say, "You see, she's the one pushing me away!"

Finally, the judge called me. She was a very nice woman in her fifties. When I saw the thin sheets of paper in her hand, I couldn't help but think: "There, ten years of my life fit in there!"

She questioned me. I was blocked, locked. My mouth was dry and I struggled to get a word out.

"So you want a divorce?

- Yes...

- You're accusing your husband of violence, aren't you?

- Yes...

- Try to tell me..."

I was afraid to cry, the words wouldn't come. I wanted to make a good impression, because I knew he'd say I was crazy, but I felt incapable, useless, stuck in my chair, looking stupid. I remembered my lawyer's words and, inwardly, I said to myself, "Speak, but just speak." I was paralyzed. But this judge was probably used to it, and had a certain discernment. She knew how to talk to me about something else, about my children I think, about the countryside where they were at the time, and she asked me if I was afraid for them. From there, she soon managed to get answers to her questions:

"What happened between you the last time you saw each other?"

I replayed the scene, the cane he'd broken on my back, how my brother had helped me get my papers back...

"Do these scenes happen often?

- All the time, well, mostly, you never know when they're going to arrive... He can also be calm and gentle..."

She was taking notes and looking at me sympathetically. Above all, she seemed to believe me, which was new to me and made it easier for me to talk after a while.

Finally, I went out and he came in.

Then she called us both back with our lawyers.

He was very comfortable. He explained that I had no intention of divorcing him, that I was psychologically fragile, that I'd gone over my head, that he was willing to forgive me...

So you're not in the wrong at all?" questioned the judge, "but I can see you got carried away... Your wife was given eight days' medical leave...

- What a joke! I barely shook her... I'm sorry about that, I really apologize, it won't happen again...

- I'm sure it wasn't the first time... You know, sir, I see men who hit their wives every day and regret it that very night!

She understood that underneath his calm, friendly façade, he was boiling. In an instant he was beside himself:

- But look at her, Judge! She's so obnoxious, she doesn't say a word on purpose, just to make people believe something...

- Perhaps she's afraid?" suggested the judge gently...

- Afraid? Of what?" he shouted so loudly that I gasped.

- Calm down!" curtly intimated the judge. Are you maintaining your request for divorce?

- Yes...

- Would you like to stay in your marital home?

He exploded:

- Certainly not, this apartment belongs to me, to my family, and if you leave, you're out of here...

- But what about the kids? They could stay in the apartment until the end of the school year, and I'd come in the evenings to look after them...

- No way," he sneered. You're out of here and that's it. You're on your own...

The judge interrupted him:

- Sir, I could very well order Madame to stay at home with the children for as long as it takes to find a place to live... I can see that you want to keep the house. What do you want, madam?

- I want the children, just custody...

- All right, then. So, sir, you keep the accommodation, madam, you keep the children... Do you know where to go? If not, I can give you a list of homes...

Of course, she told me, she could have given me the marital home, at least temporarily. But she warned me: "You know, you'll never rest easy, violent men in general are very materialistic, he won't let you go, it's better for you to go elsewhere...".

I had won. I could live alone with the kids.

He got up and left. I thanked my lawyer, who accompanied me to the exit.

"Now we're going to have to fight to get your things back, the pension, the visiting rights..."

I didn't care. I felt free.

Mom was to tell me that during the day, the children had hidden in their hut at the bottom of the garden. When she received my phone call, she went out and called them. They came running in, and she told them that the judge had granted us permission to live away from their father, and that they would be staying with me.

They were relieved.

Even so, I knew that trouble was about to take a different turn.

As his godfather had told me, he'd never been upset in his life, and now, at over 40, someone was standing up to him. He was ulcerated. From that moment on, he had only one determination: to make me pay, as dearly as possible, for what he called the destruction of his life.

He tried everything: the material argument, by becoming unemployed and stopping paying me alimony after the second month; harassment, by phoning me at home in the middle of the night and coming to wait for me at work; everything.

And then he attacked the children, using them to get at me.

I've had three difficult years, both materially and morally. Three years of hardship and fear. Because the hardest thing is not leaving, leaving everything behind, being alone. No, the hardest thing is to rebuild. To pick yourself up.

But I never, never regretted my choice. Even at the most difficult times, I said to myself: "At least I'm at peace, I'm at peace." And I fought to give that peace to my children.

I stayed with my parents for two months before moving into an OPAC apartment in the Paris region. Fortunately, they were there to help me and keep the children safe. I was very lucky to have a family by my side. I've known women who were terribly alone, who had nothing, no family, no job, and who felt doomed. I didn't even have that excuse; if I'd wanted to, I could have left much sooner, but I preferred to cling to an illusion of family. I blamed myself for that for a long time.

During the children's first vacation with their father, I called up all my friends to make the flat habitable, stripping off the old paper, repainting, washing, making up the beds, and scouring flea markets for a table, chairs and an old fridge... My children had lived in a plush Parisian apartment block up until then, so what would they think of this council apartment?

When they opened the door, they squealed with delight! They thought it was huge (of course, there was no furniture) and what's more, there was a large park downstairs. And, best of all, it was

Chapter 9

their home. They could decorate the walls, leave their shoes in the hallway, turn on the kitchen and hallway lights without getting slapped, answer the phone... Later, they would tell me it was freedom!

We were happy. The only downside was the weekends at their father's, which they dreaded from Monday onwards. I tried to condition them, telling them that their father would surely be happy to see them, that they would find their things there, and I promised them a little present on their return. In the end, I explained that they had to go. There was no other way.

The first vacations they'd spent at their father's house had been difficult. He didn't want the kids to call me.

Jean would hide to phone and whisper, "Mum, come and get us, Dad's having a fit all the time and now that you're gone, he's taking it out on me!"

I blamed myself even more. I was no longer there to distract them, to take them to the park or elsewhere. There were no cell phones in those days, and they were left to their own devices, with a father they nicknamed "the madman". Every weekend he had to pick them up, Jean would repeat that they were in "police custody"! I felt powerless to protect them. At first, I acted as I had when I was still living with their father. I gave in to his every demand, and kept quiet in the face of his demands and contradictions. He wanted to take them to school? I gave them their bags for two days. He wanted to take them home on Saturday? Had he had enough? I'd run and get them.

Again, it took me a while to understand. I thought that if I was good-natured, if I didn't upset him, things would work out for the kids. I was wrong: whatever I did, if he were to be obnoxious to the children, it wouldn't make any difference. When they were with him, it was a total blackout. I knew nothing, and the children soon realized that I was powerless.

In those days, people said it was important not to cut children off from their fathers. That a bad relationship was better than no relationship at all. How many children have been sacrificed to this principle, to these generalities that psychologists, commissioned by the courts, decided, without listening, without seeing the children's suffering!

Besides, I told myself that I had to get them to see things in a positive light. To take what was good when they were with their father. Today, I believe that when a parent is harmful, it's better to wait until the child is armed to resist the pressure. Children need to be brought up in security; only then can they confront a deficient or manipulative parent. Of course, judges can't gauge the sincerity of each individual at a glance or by reading a file. So they do the best they can, taking no risks. But it's the children who take the risks, and they too suffer the damage.

My children stayed with their father until they were about 18. Even though, from the moment we left Paris, he didn't insist as much, and no longer systematically went to the gendarmes.

They have horrible memories of those weekends. They still blame me for doing nothing to stop them going to his place.

If I'd been able to leave a thousand kilometers earlier, they would probably have suffered less and rediscovered their father as young adults. They would then have been able to defend themselves.

All I could do was run, but not far enough, not fast enough.

"Yes, you got away with it and now we have to put up with it, it's not fair," said Jean. Pauline didn't say much, but she was worried about her father: "Mom, you know, Dad's all alone, he's very sad, so we have to be nice to him, even when he's screaming..."; "I don't want to go anymore, he scares me," said Dina. She often whined, and her father, who was less at ease with her, left her to me more willingly.

How could he protect them without falling foul of a correctional procedure he was in a hurry to initiate? Non-presentation of children is a term they've heard over and over again.

"If you don't come for the weekend, I'll throw her in jail... Anyway, your mother doesn't earn enough money, she won't be able to pay the rent, you'll end up on the street..."

He terrorized them. I didn't ask them any more questions when they came home on Sundays, because I could tell they were uncomfortable, and even the slightest "Did everything go well?" I told myself that he had lived with them for almost ten years, that he knew how to look after them, that he would perhaps be more at ease without me, that he would want them to love him.

But just as our happiness didn't matter to him when we were together, the children's happiness, their pleasure in coming to see him, didn't enter into it. The children had to come because "he was entitled to them", period. He never tried to make life pleasant for them. He didn't have to make any effort: he was their father, the rest was a matter of course. And again, if they were unhappy with him, it was because I was gone, so the fault was mine. "I'm not to blame for this situation, I didn't want a divorce. If you're suffering, it's not my fault, but it would be a world apart if I had to make an effort too! Does your mother make efforts? Huh?" This leitmotiv put an end to all discussion.

Moreover, the children, at least the two older ones, were silent, careful not to provoke their father. When, years later, I asked them why they'd never said anything to me, they replied: "You couldn't help it, so there was no point in talking about it. Even the shrink, when she asked us if everything was all right, we'd say yes, because for us, this was Dad's normal situation, that's all…"

Only one judge had requested a medical-psychiatric assessment of the entire family. A great moment!

The psychologist received me first with the children, who expressed themselves quite freely. Jean explained that his father was kind but often angry, and that he didn't want to live with him all the time. Pauline, as usual, defended her lonely and sad father. Dina talked mainly about the cat and her marbles, which she spilled everywhere.

Then she saw the children with their father. They stood at attention and didn't say a word, except to nod. Even I found this attitude normal, knowing that the children had understood that they had to "be good to Dad".

She then asked to see both of us. I was afraid he'd follow me down the stairs, but the shrink assured me she'd hold him back.

"But finally, sir, you do realize that it's not good for your children the way you're reacting?" she asked him.

- But it's her fault!" he shouted, pointing at me, "if she hadn't left I wouldn't be acting like this, it's all her fault!…"

There was nothing more to say. The psychologist was as frightened by my husband's behavior as I was. He legitimized everything he did by incriminating me. I'd left, dared to leave him, abandoned him, so his revenge was justified.

He confessed to me one day:
"I'm not interested in children without you…".
And he knew just how to get to me by attacking them.

CHAPTER 10

The psychologist took a year to deliver her verdict. Namely, that he couldn't cope with all three children at the same time, and that she recommended that Jean go off on his own one weekend, and the two girls together the next. A solution we'd already tried by the time she suggested it.

But Jean didn't like going to his father's house alone, and the girls didn't interest him enough to take them without their brother.

Soon, he was poisoning our existence.

One Saturday, when he was supposed to pick them up from school, a neighbor came to me at around 1 p.m. and said: "But your children are still at school? Aren't they coming home?" I hurried over. The three of them were waiting in the rain. They hadn't dared leave. I took them home and left two messages with their father.

On Monday morning I was summoned to the gendarmerie for failure to present children. He had witnesses who testified that he was at school and that the children were not. My neighbor testified that she had seen the children waiting. But I got a sermon and another threat of correctional proceedings.

"Do you expect me to believe that your children would have waited two hours in the rain without getting home?" the policeman shouted.

Who could have believed it? The children feared their father, and if he'd told them to wait, they could have waited all day without flinching. But it was so hard to explain. He was so special and Machiavellian sometimes that I gave up trying to make people understand who he was. I knew what the answer would be. And so did the children. That's why they didn't talk. They knew it was useless.

Whereas I had previously been reluctant to use these methods, I learned to live by surrounding myself with precautions, witnesses and friends ready to defend me.

One day, a social worker was assigned to go and see how things were going with their father.

Much later, Pauline was to tell me:

"But you know, the lady, Dad knew when she was coming. He'd make us fries, and then she'd ask us questions in front of Dad, so we'd get scared, we'd say we were happy..."

"She's a lady to keep an eye on Dad," Jean had asked, "because I told her it would be nice if she stayed longer, but she just marked things in a little notebook..."

Childcare professionals, no matter how competent, have trouble detecting perversity and double-dealing. And then there was the constant reproach of the bad mother, the implication that I was an abusive mother, turning the children against the father, that poor man dispossessed of everything... Judges, social workers, shrinks, would admonish me: "Well, you have to let him have a relationship with his children, he's probably a bad husband, but maybe he's also a good father...". I lowered my head, feeling guilty and ashamed, and nodded: "Yes, that's for sure."

It took me so long to react, to regain some self-esteem. I felt guilty inflicting this separation on my children, even though I knew I was right. Children, as all childcare professionals agree, hate conflict and are always better off with separated parents than with a couple screaming at each other. Let's stop putting pressure on couples by making them believe that lasting is synonymous with proving, in everyone's eyes, that a relationship is successful. Of course, children always suffer when their parents separate. But we can't spare our children everything, even if we want to. Their parents may die, they may leave each other, they may move away, and every step of the way can cause children to suffer to a greater or lesser degree. Our responsibility as parents is not to avoid these traumas at all costs, but to accompany them and teach them how to overcome them. In fact, I felt even more guilty for having waited so long before leaving...

The father I'd given them wasn't the right one, and I'd carry this absurd feeling of failure with me for a long time.

The first time they went on vacation, he dropped them off at his mother's, who was nearly 80. After eight days, she called me in a panic:

"My dear, come and get them, I can't manage, he's gone..."

I rushed to Normandy and took my children on board, happy with this outcome.

Three days later, my lawyer called me:

"But why did you do it?" Your ex has filed a complaint for child abduction in his absence at his mother's home...

As I explained the situation, he made me swear never to go and get them again, too bad, it was too risky. How many times had my heart twisted as I listened to my son whisper to me on the phone:

"Come on, Mom, come and get us...

- I can't, you know I'm not allowed to..."

Little by little, my son lost all faith in the law and in adults, who failed to protect him.

I didn't want to speak ill of their father. When the children told me about one or other of his attitudes or actions, I remained silent. By doing so, I probably gave the impression of condoning his actions. I should have severely condemned their father's actions when they told me that he had shouted at his mother or broken things. Only now do I understand that I should have made it clear to my children that their father's behavior was wrong, but that it didn't call into question their love for him.

My son once asked me:

"But who's right, you or Daddy? Because Dad says it's your fault and you've ruined everything, and you say Dad's too angry and you can't live with him anymore..."

I procrastinated:

- You know, everyone has their own truth, it's like when you argue with your friends, everyone thinks they're right...

But Jean, with his childlike logic, insisted:

- Yes, but I want to know who started it!"

Weekends at his father's were to provide some of the answers.

I myself was having trouble recovering from ten years of living with my husband. For years, I'd taken the same route home, and it took me a long time to stop taking the wrong metro. Sometimes I'd find myself on the platform and, out of habit, I'd go back in the old direction. At night I'd dream I was going back there, hear the keys jingling in the crystal bowl in the hallway, the closet creaking.

I'd wake up with a start, convinced that I could feel him on the edge of the bed, that I could smell his wheezing as his anger rose like an ocean of rage. His chopped-up words echoing in my eardrums, I turned on the light, to regain my footing in reality, in my bed, alone, in the room stripped of furniture.

When I got home from work, I'd feel so oppressed that I'd sit down for a few minutes and try to calm myself down. I'd lived so much under stress, so afraid of going home, that I had to make an effort, convince myself that I was safe before opening my door and finding the kids.

In the same way, as the evening wore on, I could feel the anxiety building. I'd say to myself: "Quick, quick, the bath, dinner"; and suddenly I'd stop: "But calm down, he's not going to come in here, you're at home, there's no more danger..."

What a joy to leave things lying around in the hallway, to chat with the children quietly without worrying about a strict schedule, to prepare pasta and eat it sitting with them, laughing. The quiet of an evening when I could tuck the kids in and sit by their beds, listen to their little stories, take a bath, read in bed. Simple things that had never been part of my life.

Little by little I regained a little calm. He got tired of waiting for me when I got off work, stopped making phone calls at night, and stopped sending me threatening letters.

He paid alimony every other month, and our contacts were reduced to the bare minimum. I was so relieved to feel him moving away from me that I refused to fight for the money he owed the children. He gave when he wanted. As he soon saw that I wasn't starting any proceedings, the financial weapon eventually lost its value and he started paying again, after having the sum reduced to the minimum.

Some people didn't understand, telling me "But fight for the children, you can't live and toil at work when he should be helping you, the children are his too...". But I preferred not to make things worse, not to restart the legal machine. Cowardice no doubt, but I didn't have enough energy left to fight this battle.

I continued to work at my second job, at night, so I could barely make ends meet. But these financial difficulties really wore me down. Even now, I still dread the end of the month, so I go back over my accounts and put money aside. I still find it hard to spend money on myself, as if I didn't have the right to do so, as if what I could buy for my own pleasure was deducted from my children's. I love shopping, but it's not always easy. I like to go shopping, but with my daughters, and I'm reluctant to treat myself to anything superfluous. A sign of a time when paying for the canteen was a real feat. The children suffered because they could see I was struggling with bills, the bank...

The second year, the children didn't want to go away with their father for a month. He agreed to take the girls for only a fortnight, but refused to take Jean. He had planned to take him camping on his own. However, he refused to pick him up and wanted him to take the train alone. My lawyer suggested that Jean be heard by the judge to explain that he was willing to go with his father, but not for a whole month.

This time we had no luck. The judge told us straight away that she was going on vacation and had a train to catch.

"Come to an agreement with your lawyers, I don't want to hear this child anyway, he's 11, he's too young...

- But, Madam Judge," I tried to explain, "he's still very traumatized, and he's very apprehensive about going alone with his father...

She looked at me and replied:

- I mean, he hasn't killed him yet, has he? You're exaggerating..."

Jean rolled around the room, shouting that he wouldn't go with his father.

Our lawyers decided that Jean would join his father for a fortnight, and that he would bring him back to me on August 16.

"But what if Dad doesn't give me back?" he worried.

- I'll come and get you, I promise, wherever you are, I'll come...

- Why didn't the judge listen to me? I would have explained to her what Dad does when he's angry... "

My father took Jean to Toulouse and put him on the train to Tarbes with a telephone card and a thousand recommendations.

He didn't phone to let us know he'd arrived; his father had confiscated his card. I was worried sick. Finally, my mother-in-law called secretly to say everything was fine.

And on August 16, no one.

I knew he was in our house in the Vendée: the neighbors and my sister-in-law had seen his car. But not the little boy, whom his father hid away, forbidding him to go out and show himself. For two days, this child lived locked up, for fear of being spotted. No beach, no garden, nothing.

My sister-in-law spotted him one morning, sitting alone on the front steps.

"Are you okay?" she worried.

- Yes...

He whispered fearfully.

- Do you want me to call Mom?" she asked, also half aloud.

Jean turned his head and nodded. Then his father called him and he ran off.

As soon as my sister-in-law announced: "He's here, I've seen him", I didn't hesitate for a second. I'd promised her I wouldn't let him down, so I had to go.

My brother J.-P. came with me. We left very early in the morning. By eleven o'clock, we were there. The car was parked in the garden, out of sight. I still didn't know how I was going to get there.

My neighbor greeted me with a wave: "They're here," she said, before heading home.

So I opened the wicket and went downstairs. They were around the table, pulled into the recess near the kitchen.

Later, Jean was to tell me, "When I saw you arrive, Mom, on the terrace, it was like an apparition!"

His father was taken aback. "I've come to fetch Jean," I simply announced before taking my son by the hand. By the time he got up and threw himself on top of me, we had run to the car, and my brother had stepped in.

We started up again right away. I was relieved to have kept my word. I wanted Jean to know that I wouldn't let him down. On the way home, Jean trembled whenever a police car appeared. My brother finally reassured him: "Look, Jean, we haven't done anything wrong. Your father should have brought you back two days ago; he's the one who did wrong by hiding you away like that!"

His father was in the wrong, there was nothing he could do. No matter how hard he tried, no matter how much he yelled through his lawyer, he knew he should have put his son back on the train. He was furious because, deep down, he didn't believe I was capable of going against his wishes. I wouldn't have believed myself capable of it, but a few months out of his clutches had given me back an energy I'd thought gone forever. Having said that, even though the courts were quick to accuse me of not having children, they took no action against him for failing to return our son on time, despite the handrail I had sent to my lawyer.

I felt stronger. I knew I'd made my point. He couldn't believe that I'd dared to come between him and Jean, that I hadn't given in. A step had been taken, and if he always took them at the whim of his mood, at least afterwards he always returned them to me on time. Here again, the law is strange, since my lawyer had explained to me: "Look, he has the right to take them according to the terms of the judgement, but it's not an obligation; if he doesn't take them, there's nothing to say…".

Of course, when in the end he didn't come for them, we were relieved and the weekend looked good. But there was still the tension of waiting and the painful feeling of being at his mercy again and again.

This is the way the law works, giving fathers many rights and the only obligation they have is to make regular pension payments.

CHAPTER 11

I thought I was gradually becoming less afraid of him. In truth, I was content to keep him at a distance. I didn't let him get to me any more, because between two fights, I could lift my head out of the water, out of his grip, I could take a breath of strength, of freedom, and I could act again.

But as soon as I saw him, as soon as I heard his voice, the old demons awoke. I could feel my limbs tense up; I could feel my brain go numb, shutting itself behind an irrational fear. I'd become a block of stone again, a ball of anguish, and my reactions would escape me like soap bubbles that I could see flying away endlessly. I watched helplessly as I was asphyxiated and killed. It was as if I had become a spectator of my own life.

The hardest part isn't leaving, living in difficult conditions, raising children alone. No, the hardest thing is to forget your fears and anxieties, like useless old masks. At the slightest shock, they pop up like ghosts and paralyze reality.

We have to tell ourselves every day that we're a person of value, that we're entitled to respect, that people can love us, that we're going to succeed, that we have the right to express ourselves. To become a whole person, not just a being in perdition, preoccupied only with survival and the next minute.

Shortly after the separation, I had spoken with a friend and confided in him my fear of not getting out of it. He smiled and said: "But that's it, you're out of it... Now you just have to follow your path without looking back..."

Even today, I'm afraid of conflict, of raising my voice, of making brutal gestures. I find it hard to impose my point of view on people close to me, because I'm afraid of the anger that could devastate everything. I have less difficulty in my professional environment because, on the one hand, I have less to lose in terms of relationships and, on the other, my skills have been less scorned. No matter how much my husband criticized my work, I knew I was getting results, that I was appreciated.

I believe that women who don't work are even more vulnerable when they're under a hold. Not only because they have a financial dependence that's hard to overcome, but also because they have nothing, no network to hold on to in order to blossom, to leave open a door to a self that might have value. They are denied everything and end up losing all confidence. A job is a lifeline, and not just a financial one. I think mothers really need to get this idea into their daughters' heads.

Years later, I had a rather hot-tempered boss and we often disagreed. One day, he came shouting at me and I instinctively raised my elbow to protect myself. A reflex that left him speechless. He stopped shouting at me and left the room. I was ashamed of my attitude, feeling betrayed by my body, vulnerable and at the same time so ridiculous! As if my boss was going to hit me!... Force of habit and fear rooted in the deepest recesses of my mind.

I'm proud that I had the courage to leave, despite the way others looked at me and the misunderstandings. People like him are very clever, and public opinion is always to their advantage. They are versatile but intelligent personalities, who know how to show a part of themselves that conforms to what is expected. But I think that if I'd been older, I wouldn't have had the necessary strength. A few more years and I would have resigned myself to a life without joy, a life of permanent terror. I would have been broken when I was still just shaken and distraught.

I still had strength because I had this love for my children, I had hope and I didn't want this life for them. Today, I know that I made mistakes, that sometimes I acted stupidly, but never, never did I say to myself that it would have been better for me to stay with their father. And they never said that to me either.

I probably didn't really love this man. I was secure with him, he offered me a model for my life that I knew how to use, and I admired him. But there was never any tenderness or complicity between us. Just a power struggle.

It took twelve years to break the rope that kept me chained. That's a lot of time. It's too much. But the worst thing would have been to stay in the wrong, not to make mistakes. I was wrong for a long time, but I finally realized it, and I think I realized it in time.

But the children endured five years of weekends in "police custody", as Jean used to say. And I tried to live again, to rebuild myself, which took some time. Almost twenty years.

Firstly, because if you leave your partner, it's pointless expecting any sympathy. If I had left, it was my decision, and in the eyes of many, it was hard to understand why I was unhappy about it. But I was unhappy. On the one hand, because the material conditions in which I found myself (alone with three children and a civil servant's salary) were difficult. But also because I had to mourn my marriage, my life, the one I had supported for over ten years.

Soon, I stopped explaining and justifying myself. I let people imagine what suited them. That he was the one who'd left, that we'd agreed. My ex-husband, on the other hand, spent two years laying siege to my friends, telling them nonsense about me. That I was crazy, fragile, that I should be locked up, that the children should be taken away from me, that I had stolen money and possessions from him... He followed me around, making threats. I went into hiding. I never went out at the same time. I took different routes. It was exhausting, because again, I was under a lot of pressure.

A friend lent me her car one weekend to take the kids to a show. They were delighted. Did they tell their father about it? I didn't want to tell them: "Don't say this, don't say that"; I found it disturbing. Anyway, by Sunday morning, all four tires were slashed... He was sniggering on the sidewalk across the street. It was his way of demonstrating that he still had the power to harm me.

A few months later, I ran into a mutual friend. She asked me kindly: "How are you? I've heard about your troubles..." Thinking she was talking about the divorce, I thanked her and started the conversation. Suddenly she interrupted me, embarrassed: "No, but what about you? How are you? Are you seeing the kids again? I was taken aback. My ex-husband had told our friends that he'd had to have me committed for depression and that he was taking care of the children on his own... I didn't know what to say to set the record straight, and I'm not sure she believed me.

Above all, my material difficulties clouded my horizon, kept me awake at night and absorbed all my energy. When he arranged to pay the alimony every other month, which exempted him from prosecution, the children would come home from their father's house saying: "You know, Mom, Dad doesn't have any money, you take everything from him, so he can't buy us food when we come, and you have plenty in the fridge!"

I was annoyed, but what could I tell them? They finally understood, as they grew up.

When I worked nights, from 11 p.m. to 7 a.m., I'd call Jean and give him my number. I'd leave when they were asleep. My neighbor upstairs would come down to have a look. Here again, I was lucky to live in a housing estate where many civil servants, like me, lived, but also a number of single-parent families, single mothers who formed a solid network. How many times did my children sleep over at a neighbor's while I took hers, in exchange, on summer vacations?

I'd get home before they got up, get them ready and go back to work with them. Fortunately, I was young and healthy enough to hold down two jobs...

For a long time, I thought his problem was giving money to me. When Jean turned 20, he offered to pay her alimony directly. I agreed, thinking it would be better and simpler. But as my son did not go on to higher education, he stopped paying it two months later, arguing that his studies alone warranted help[1]. He contented himself with giving him a little money from time to time, but it was always a worry, a complaint, and Jean didn't dare talk to me about it.

His story was a lesson to his sisters. When he repeated the idea to the majority of the girls, they refused: "You understand, Mom, he's

---

1. At the time, the law stipulated that the pension was payable "until completion of regular education", whereas today it is paid until "financial independence".

obliged to pay you, and we don't want to spend our time asking him for anything...".

I didn't want them to have to sue their father either.

Those years in Paris were exhausting. We didn't live in the same neighborhood, but he would walk the children home on Sunday evenings, almost four kilometers by eight o'clock, to save on metro fares. I knew better than to start a controversy.

Saying nothing, feigning indifference when he cut the children's socks (because they were worn out and I'd have to buy new ones), when he forbade them to phone me for homework, when he "forgot" to bring in a schoolbag, a source of anguish for them on Monday mornings.

I played the same game he did. I'd say to the kids: "Oh, I'm so glad you're going to spend a fortnight at Dad's this All Saints' Day! I'm going to take a trip during that time..." (Obviously, I didn't have the time or the money for that.)

Jean immediately understood the message and was quick to repeat it to his father. I was sure he wouldn't take them on vacation, or only for a few days. The girls had also got the message. In the evenings, all three of them at their father's house, they would say to little Dina: "Are you sad? Do you want to see Mommy?" Of course, Dina would burst into tears and cry "Mommy"...

Their father wasn't very comfortable with her. He didn't know her very well, since he'd moved away shortly after she was born, and she was barely 4 when we split up. After a while, Jean would say gravely: "You know, Dad, I think she's sick...".

Their father would end up calling me and I'd come and get them... Sick, the children knew they had a good chance of not going to their father's house. They too learned how to get away from him, using his phobias.

Eventually, the children settled into this new life. They had friends, a calm environment and their father ended up spacing out the unannounced visits, the guilt-ridden phone calls, and taking them away less at weekends.

Soon, I wasn't taking the wrong metro line home, and I wasn't looking for the things I'd left at home. Sometimes, even today, when I see a knick-knack or a coffee set in a store, I say to myself: "Well, I had this or that, where is it? Until I realize that these objects belonged to me in another life."

I hadn't collected anything because, at the time of the partition, on the date and at the time set by the judge, my brother and a few friends went to ring the apartment bell. He never opened the door, but indicated through the door that my things were in the cellar.

He'd thrown away my clothes and a few of the kids' toys. That was all. What could I do? Call a bailiff? It would have been expensive and I wasn't even sure of the result.

At first I missed these things, but now I've forgotten they even existed. I don't even know what's left in this apartment.

We lived on very little, I furnished myself with odds and ends with the help of my parents, and I was happy.

One day, for her birthday, Pauline invited her classmates and her second grade teacher, whom she adored. In my living room, I had a bed strewn with colorful cushions, a table made of a plank and two trestles, and an Ikea shelf with a TV on the floor. The teacher exclaimed: "How nice! Did you push all the furniture into another room for her birthday party?"

I didn't dare say it was all I had...

But the children had no regrets. They loved this apartment, in which they felt at home and at ease.

A new life had begun.

I was promoted in my job. As the children got older, they became more independent. With everyone's help, I got organized.

And I met someone who lit up my life. I realized, with this new relationship, that I'd never known what it really meant to be loved. Without criticism, without judgment, without blame. Just for who I was.

Chapter 12

I wasn't yet able to really trust, to let myself go. I only wanted to rely on myself, so afraid was I of being at the mercy of a tyrant again. I realized that I saw all men as potential dangers, and I could feel how disturbing my attitude sometimes was. But I couldn't help it. The men I met were rarely free, which suited me, I didn't feel capable of starting a new life as a couple.

And then one day, I felt I could trust someone again. Relative trust, in fact, because for a while, I didn't want to let go of anything, I wanted to take charge of my whole life. Not to depend on someone, even if I loved them.

When we decided to leave Paris, I kept my apartment for three years, just in case... I was afraid I'd have to come back in a hurry with the children, and I needed this security, this fallback solution. Making the decision to ask for a transfer to Toulouse, taking the children once again into another life, was a real turning point.

I'd lost my self-confidence, I was afraid of making another mistake, and I was more than ever afraid of dragging the children into a complicated adventure. At the same time, I told myself that it couldn't be any worse than what I'd been through...

Somehow, the ordeal of the divorce had made me stronger. I'd got through it, and felt strengthened in the idea that I could face any situation as long as I'd escaped from HIM. So why not try to be happy?

I knew that my ex-husband would take it badly and that he'd give me a hard time. I also knew that establishing a geographical distance could only be beneficial. I had a vague feeling that the moral distance was there between us, but that these kilometers would mark a final and decisive point.

After sending him a letter (registered, of course), we moved to Toulouse. I was anxious, I wasn't sure of anything, but I knew it would be better.

Time was also on my side. My son was 15, and we could no longer throw him in the back of the car like a bundle and force him to go to his father's for the weekend. Little by little, he got out of the physical grip because he was growing up.

One Saturday evening, one of the last times he had to go alone to his father's house before we left, I found Jean quietly watching TV as I returned from shopping. He didn't look worried or annoyed, just told me he was home. Believing it to be a last-minute whim of their father's, I didn't worry too much. It was while listening to my answering machine, an hour later, that I became aware of his father's calls. Furious and worried, he said he didn't know where his son had gone.

"Jean, what exactly happened with Dad?

My son shrugged:

- Well, nothing, as usual, he started shouting for nothing and stuck me at the door on the landing... So I went home..."

I picked up the phone to reassure his father, who was obviously on a roll: "Come on, he's 15! What do you expect? His days of crying behind the door are over! He knows how to take the metro and get home!"

That was the last time he would indulge in this kind of behavior with his son.

Jean was also beginning to stand between his father and his sisters physically, and the corporal bullying was likely to fade, but not the vexations and humiliations...

The girls would later tell me that they often spent their evenings on the landing, in their pyjamas, being punished. Around midnight, it was not unusual for Sylvie, the neighbor, to send them home, or to ring the doorbell of their father, who had forgotten them or was asleep in front of the TV.

It was time to move away.

We arrived in Toulouse in July, and the summer passed without any news of their father.

In September, I received a summons from the gendarmerie. Non-presentation of children. He claimed not to know where they were. My lawyer forwarded a copy of my registered letter to him, with our address on it. And reminded him that he had to send the train tickets for the outward journey (I was paying for the return) if he wanted to take the children.

That was the last time he took me to court. Little by little, the stranglehold loosened, like a cloud that had been constantly hanging over my life and was finally dissipating.

I owed this respite to his remarriage.

As his second wife was from Narbonne, he would occasionally pass through Toulouse and see the children for ten minutes in the parking lot. Yet sometimes they were reluctant to come down and say hello. My companion tried once to convince Jean:

"Come on, it'll be fun, your dad'll take you for a walk, you'll go for a drink..."

Jean, knowing his father, was doubtful. He eventually went, taking his sisters with him, and returned an hour later:

- Well?" my friend asked.

Jean shrugged:

- Well, we stayed in the car, dad had a bad back and showed us his X-rays...

And off he went to play with his friends. My friend was appalled and said:

- You see, I've never questioned your word, but things like this, if I hadn't heard your son talk about them, I'd find it hard to believe... His father comes to see them for ten minutes and all he can do is complain..."

For about three years, we had peace and quiet. The children even spent a few vacations in Narbonne with their mother-in-law, who was very kind to them. I was relieved to know that someone had managed to tame my ex-husband. The vacations and the time the children spent with them seemed calm and they seemed happy. She would take them to the beach, eat ice-cream, and then, with their father having a new life, he took them less often, which was a relief to them. In fact, these were practically the only times their father took them without drama. He probably wanted to make a good impression on his in-laws.

I learned to breathe, I learned to distance myself, I learned to forget. As children grew up, they dealt with their relationship, or lack of it, with their father.

My life was brightening up again and starting to take shape in the South-West. I had changed jobs and was passionate about my work.

I had almost no contact with my ex-husband, and it was the girls who told me one day that a little sister was going to be born in their father's home.

I think they were happy, even though my son began by resenting his father: "He's remarried, he didn't tell us, he's got a baby, we're only finding out now! It sucks!..."

I think deep down he wasn't sure how to tell them...

This little sister remained an unknown for a long time. Their father refused to receive them at first, claiming his wife was tired. In reality, their marriage had deteriorated from birth. What the children told me when their father finally allowed them to come suggested that he was at it again, as temperamental and violent as ever.

You understand," said my son, "as long as she wasn't under his control, it was fine, but now, with the baby, she's in his clutches... I told her not to stay with Dad, but she wouldn't listen to me..."

Who do you listen to when you think you're starting a family? Certainly not a 15-year-old boy... I told my son to stay out of it, and life would take its course.

I was working a lot and didn't have the time or inclination to deal with my ex-husband's affairs. Yet I could feel that he could still get to me sometimes. When the children would come back from their few hours together in the parking lot and talk about his delirious speeches, when he would tell Dina he wanted to see her on vacation, then, at the last minute, cancel the trip, leaving her inconsolable. As long as the children were old enough to go to his house, when I felt they were at his mercy, a part of my heart still worried. Moreover, in case anything happened to me, I had drawn up a will, filed with a notary. In the event of my death, I asked that my children be entrusted to my parents: "At least," my lawyer explained, "instead of going directly to their father, we can convene a family council and take your last wishes into account...".

When Jean turned 18, I had the will changed so that he would be the guardian of his sisters.

All these years, I kept a deep-rooted feeling of anxiety. When he came to see the children, I didn't leave my house, for fear of running into him; when I took the children to the train, I let them go ahead on the platform, and waited to see them leave with him. I trembled at the thought of approaching him.

Years later, he phoned one evening. He rarely called since he knew I no longer lived alone. But hearing his voice was like an electric shock; I could barely get two words out to put one of the kids on the phone.

I resented this attitude. I tried to reason with myself, but deep down, what upset me most was realizing this recurring fear. Despite my happy life, despite the man by my side who reassured me, I was furious that his voice alone still frightened me. I was angry at myself for not being cured. Because he'd left me alone, he'd rebuilt his life and was tired of ruining me. But I had this vague feeling that everything could start again. That the distance wasn't enough, firstly because, despite everything, the children were still young and still relied on me to come between them and their father. I tried to get them to deal with their relationship with their father on their own, but they refused for a long time. I think they saw it as my duty to stand between them and their father, and felt, as Jean used to say, that "it was up to me to deal with him".

"You're the one who gave us this father, it's up to you now..."

And then, less than a year after the birth of their half-sister, my ex-husband's marriage exploded.

CHAPTER 13

When I saw history repeat itself, with my children's half-sister, I was overwhelmed by anger, sadness and a feeling of powerlessness.

This little girl lived less with her father because the second wife, smarter than me, stayed with him for barely two years. She quickly fled with her daughter under her arm, escaping beatings and insults, leaving her job to take refuge with her parents on the other side of France.

The children experienced their father's second divorce as a second trauma. For my part, this separation challenged me. The children spoke very highly of their stepmother, and the fact that the violence resurfaced legitimized my actions and relieved me of some of my guilt: if he started up again with her, then it wasn't all my fault. I realize today that this thought is a little ridiculous, but it's proof that after so many years, I was still carrying on my shoulders what I thought was a failure. In the light of this second fiasco, my story seemed legitimate. But then I realized that, up to that point, I hadn't marked the end of the story.

While I was relieved and unconcerned about what would happen next, the children were worried about the little girl. And I could see that attitudes had changed little in fifteen years. Fathers are more assertive in asserting their rights, mothers are still fighting for unpaid child support, and children are no more listened to today than they were yesterday.

I've heard the following: "Listening to a child is likely to traumatize him if he has to decide between his father and mother…"; "The child repeats what the parent he spends most time with says" (often the mother); "The child must see both parents equally" (for supporters of alternating custody); "It's the courts who decide, it's better for the child…". It's as if abusive parents don't exist. Or very few.

A child with a deviant parent will be traumatized, that's for sure. But who takes responsibility for saying this, and especially for writing it down? No one does. My son has seen several doctors, pediatricians and child psychiatrists who have testified that he was distressed by the idea of going to his father's house, but the courts have never taken this into account.

Would it be possible to set up training courses for magistrates in charge of family affairs and childcare professionals to teach them how to recognize perverts? To be able to put a name to these forms of violence, which are so particular that they leave no visible, immediate traces, but a destructive, indelible mark?

There are abusive, manipulative, perverse mothers. What I'm denouncing is not exclusive to men. But it seems to me that we would gain in speed if we studied the attitude of the partner in these families. If a woman appears weakened, lost, without self-esteem, afraid of everything, unable to find arguments to justify herself, perhaps she's the victim of a pervert. And if the man seems affable, down-to-earth, slightly protective and magnanimous, with children at attention at his side, it may be worth checking to see if he's easily angered or reproached.

One of the judges with whom we were confronted immediately understood my husband's character. In two sentences she got him off his duff and, throwing caution to the wind, he showed his true colors. He recovered quickly, but it was too late. She had realized the magnitude of the problem. Unfortunately, few people know how to lift the mask and bring the wolf out of its den. But it's probably possible to learn how to detect perversity...

My children's little sister first saw her father in a children's home, a neutral, somewhat protected place. Her father would ask Jean to come with him, as he didn't feel up to going alone. Besides, he must have felt humiliated. Eventually, he stopped going.

But when the child grew up, he managed to regain normal visiting rights. The child was anxious to spend time with her father, and as my son used to say: "She's all alone, no one's defending her...".

Her mother tried to take her away from this dreaded vacation, and ended up with a criminal conviction. Resigned, she tried, as I used to do, to condition her daughter by explaining that the week would go by quickly, and that she'd have a present when she got back.

For this little girl, the hell continued.

My children became even more worried about their little sister when she was forced to go alone to her father's house in Paris. She must have been 7 or 8 years old, her mother would put her on a plane to Marseille, and she would spend weeks at a time with her father, whom she hardly knew and who terrorized her.

There were three of us, but now she's all alone and her mother's eight hundred miles away!" insisted Jean.

- And Pauline added: "We're used to Dad, but she's hardly seen him...".

It wasn't my story, it wasn't my business and I didn't really want to hear about it. Until the day my mother called me.

She, unlike me, had chosen to fight to free her daughter from her father's violence, and I felt she was ready for anything. I, who had opted for resignation, I, who had left my children to endure painful weekends and vacations, couldn't help but find her courageous in her determination. Moreover, unlike my own children who had lived with their father for ten years, she didn't have a history of childhood conflict, and her father's aggressive comments left her speechless and stunned. But unlike mine, she knew that her father's attitude was unacceptable.

I proposed to use the minutes of my judgment, but these documents were declared inadmissible. I then wrote an affidavit stating that I had divorced her on the grounds of violence, in which I also confirmed that my children had had a pleasant mother-in-law, that she was a good, loving and caring mother in their opinion. My eldest daughter herself attested to this. But the judges no doubt felt that I was settling an old score (fifteen years old, after all), and the affidavits went unheeded.

Here again, I wonder what keeps the justice system from comparing stories that are repeated within a family, and what pushes it to always start from the basic assumption that the mother is exaggerating and that the child is being manipulated and cannot be believed.

Why, when my children were grown up and ready to explain their fears, did no judge ever want to hear them to untangle this family skein? Is it easier to believe a man who says the women in his life are crazy, hysterical and not to be trusted? Is it complicated, before deciding to apply a usual custody arrangement, to consult the immediate environment, which advises against accommodation if not visitation rights?

Seeking to understand is not the primary vocation of justice. No, justice is based on facts that seem intangible. Judges give the impression of being tired of divorce and family conflicts. They have reading grids that enable them to impose decisions that are, most of the time, in nobody's interest.

And in the end, the law is often on the side of the person acting in bad faith, because it's very difficult to fight against them.

My ex-husband lamented, "My wife left me and now the kids don't want to come and see me, it's so unfair."

To which the judges replied: "Of course, you have the right to see your children, but the conflict with your wife must not interfere with your paternal rights...".

On the other hand, when he knowingly paid child support every other month, no one questioned his paternal love. I was told that if he didn't pay for two months in a row, we could intervene, but of course, at the end of the second month, he paid. How was I supposed to get by for the whole month without a pension? It was a mystery. Nobody was interested.

With the little girl, he applied the same methods. His mother was supposedly depressed (and with what she'd been through, there would have been reason to be!), his family had turned her against him (one wonders why), the little girl needed a father, he loved her and was unjustly deprived of one...

When the child was 12, she told her maternal grandfather that she would kill herself if she had to return to her father's house ever again. There had been painful scenes between them, and she couldn't take it anymore. Her mother decided to have her heard by a judge and a doctor. She appointed a lawyer to represent her interests. But administrative slowness being what it is, she was told that she absolutely had to introduce her daughter to her father, or risk a criminal conviction.

It took a year, a psychological investigation and a summary judgement, before the courts paid lip service to reducing visitation rights. Knowing that the little girl lived eight hundred kilometers away and that her father had to pay for the plane tickets, he finally gave up. However, at regular intervals (no doubt in line with his crises) he would call on his daughter out of the blue, just two days before the vacations. What anguish for her, who trembled before each vacation, fearing that she would receive a plane ticket and be obliged to go to her father's!

What was in it for him? What was taken into consideration? Today, people claim that the child's voice is heard, but I'm not so sure.

I believe that if a mother unjustly takes a child away from his father, the child will resent his mother, and the day will come when he will want to know the truth for himself. But a child who has been subjected to his father's abuse throughout his childhood, and has terrible memories of it, will lose faith in human justice and in his parents for good. What's more, they run the risk of losing their bond with the parent in question forever.

If my children had seen less of their father, their childhood would undoubtedly have been more serene and perhaps, as adults, they would have wanted to meet him. They would then have been better equipped to face him as he is, and for them, for their equilibrium, things would certainly have gone better.

Today, none of my children see their father, even though he lives in the same town.

Can't their sister learn from their example?

Apparently not.

The courts don't look that far, and are content to take up the story at a given moment, without knowing how it came about. This child had to go to her father, and that was that. She did not hesitate to explain herself to the family court judge, but to no avail.

So one day, the child decided the story had gone on long enough. Since no one was coming to her aid, she repeated her threat to put herself in danger: "If I go under a car, I'll go to hospital and I won't be able to go to Daddy's...".

To this day, despite these terrible words, nothing has been decided. She hasn't gone back to her father's, but the possibility of a return trip still looms over her vacation.

Will she have to commit the irreparable, as she promised, to be heard?

Chapter 14

The story of my ex-husband's second girlfriend and their daughter made me realize that Dina had never really had an explanation for our divorce. She was 4 at the time of the separation and, while I had never excluded her from discussions, I had never addressed her in age-appropriate terms to explain the situation. As her father had demanded less of her than her brother and sister, she idealized him a little, and I let her say so. I was surprised one day to hear her say, "Why can't Daddy see our sister except in a children's home? Would he hurt her?"

When I explained to her that I'd divorced her for violence with emergency measures, she seemed astonished. My son intervened: "Yes, Mom, of course, Dina always says 'Dad's very nice' and you never say anything. Well, now she understands, but it's a bit late... We've been to Dad's house so many times that we know he's anything but nice!"

In the end, it's very difficult to choose one attitude or another with the certainty of not making a mistake. The two older ones went to live with their father, under duress, and resented it. And my youngest, whom I thought would be calmer with me, is suffering in the end because she doesn't know her father and her opinion is influenced.

Preoccupied with his divorce, their father left my children alone. They simply took advantage of my family's visits to Paris to drop in on their father from time to time.

I thought I was rid of my demons, until the day my eldest daughter left to study in Paris. For ten years, I had never had the alimony (one hundred and fifty euros per month) re-evaluated, even though the judgement provided for an annual re-evaluation based on the cost of living. Pauline urged me to take legal action: "Mom, there's no reason for you to pay for everything...".

We asked for an extra fifty euros. On the date of the hearing, Pauline accompanied me to the courthouse in Toulouse.

"You know, Dad said he'd come..."

My legs felt like absorbent cotton, my heart was pounding. Confined to the tiny waiting room, crammed in with a crowd of stressed-out people, I did my best not to let my anxiety show. And above all, I didn't understand. I hadn't seen him in ten years, I knew for a fact he couldn't do me any harm, I wasn't even sure he was coming: so where did this uneasiness come from? This feeling of running out of air with every breath, this head emptied of all arguments, the heart pounding in my stomach and preventing me from thinking clearly?

The imprint he'd left on my brain seemed indelible. Finally, the anxieties he'd poured into me and that I'd kept buried, on a leash, in a corner of my heart and guts, these anxieties could resurface at any moment.

When the time came, the judge called me and I realized he wasn't there. A lawyer was representing him, barely familiar with the case and mixing up the children's names. The judge agreed to my request, and within ten minutes we were outside.

"I was scared to death of seeing him too..." Pauline had to say.

I still had some work to do on myself. I signed up for discussion groups with women who had suffered violence. The recurrence of anguish was our common lot. Sharing these sufferings and realizing that I wasn't the only one trying to forget a painful past comforted me. A psychologist once told me: "You mustn't forget your past, you must accept it, and then move on to the future...".

Little by little, I stopped feeling guilty. I stopped feeling like a loser when my anxieties came flooding in. I went through these moments as if shrouded in fog. I knew I was heading for the sun.

It had been nearly ten years since I had undertaken this therapy, too busy beforehand mobilizing my energy to live, to get back on my feet. I took this new battle head-on, like a second chance I didn't want to let slip away. I was in love, I wanted to be happy. I didn't want to weigh on my partner, to remain mired in my irrational anxieties. I realized that after all these years, despite my blossoming and the serenity I thought I'd found, I was still afraid of the other person's gaze and unfit for any kind of commitment.

It took him nine years after the divorce was finalized for us to finally get married.

And if I'm able to write these lines, it's because this story is definitely part of the past, a difficult past, but one that has shaped the person I've become. I claim responsibility, but I no longer feel guilty. My children are grown up and have made their own way, each with their own truth, their own appreciation.

I sometimes say to my husband, "It's too bad we didn't meet sooner."

He always replies: "But it wasn't the right time earlier...".

The man I met when I was 20 accompanied me for more than ten years, gave me my children, pushed me to complete my studies and develop in my work. The suffering I endured transformed me from a naive, trusting kid into a responsible, combative adult.

As I read these lines, my son humorously said to me, "All in all, you can thank Dad!"

I don't thank him, but I don't deny him. He's no longer part of my life, but he's still an episode in my story. This is how my life was written, with this person by my side. That was the time of the worst. Then came the best, which I was able to welcome, perhaps because I'd been through a lot.

Today, the page has really been turned. I no longer hold any grudges, just indifference and sometimes a little pity for him. Because of his outbursts, he missed out on his professional life, his two marriages and his role as a father. It's a pity, but I know I couldn't do anything about it. Nobody could.

My children have left home, they live in Paris and could see their father. When I asked for a pension for Dina, so that she could continue her studies like her sister, at first he dragged it out for a year. Then the judge said:

"Your ex-husband complains that he has to pay for children he no longer sees, he points out that you are turning them against him.

- But come on, Judge, our three children live in Paris, they don't live with me anymore, do you really think that if they don't see their father it's always my fault?"

The judge nodded and granted my request.

I knew I was truly healed, liberated, because this time I wasn't afraid to meet him.

Some time ago, I moved house, and I said to myself: "I don't need to give him my address, I no longer have any contact with him, the children are grown up, the only contact left was at the boarding house, and today that's over...".

Lately, he'd been paying very regularly. Deep down, he must have felt that this was the only, the last link between us. I was relieved when that link was broken, as if the book of our history had been closed for good.

A friend once replied: "But you'll always have a bond with him, he's the father of your children...". To which I replied: "No, for me the bond is attachment. He has a bond with my children, my children have a bond with him, but there's no longer any bond between us. The children no longer need us to manage their relationship."

I think that if I saw him in the street, I wouldn't recognize him (and he probably wouldn't either), and this indifference is no longer shaded by resentment. Dina once asked me: "Would you be sad if Dad died?" I tried to be as honest as possible: "It's always sad to hear of someone's death. I'd be sad for you, of course, but at the same time, I don't think I'd feel sorry for him..."

I think I'd feel worse if I lost a colleague: there's no longer any feeling between us, and what happens to him no longer concerns me.

Pauline got married last year. I told her she could invite her father. I know I'm capable of seeing him again, of dealing with him, because I've evolved and also because I have someone at my side who loves and supports me.

She didn't want to: "You know, Dad, I haven't seen him for ten years, there's no point, and then it'll be anguish, I don't want to..."

It's true that he's certainly always unpredictable and a source of tension. But I could have accepted his presence, just as I could have accepted the presence of an irascible old uncle who has to be invited. I didn't want my daughter to be deprived of her father's presence to protect me. Children are entitled to both parents in these circumstances. I left her free to do as she pleased.

Her father-in-law led her to the altar.

As I watched her take her turn in this adventure, I thought back to the testamentary paper I'd left at the notary's office. Looking up at the blue sky, I realized that the will was obsolete. They were all of age and, more importantly, their lives were beginning, and they no longer needed me to protect them.

As I listened to the bells ringing out my daughter's happiness, I thought about how much less afraid I was of death. I could finally live life to the full.

And write this book.

By way of epilogue...

In the end, how do you get out of it? First of all, you mustn't exhaust your energy, you mustn't wait until you're no longer able to get up in the morning, no longer able to distinguish the good times from the bad. Each one has its limit, some will take ten years, others ten months, there are no rules. But there are identified phases, and having discussed them with a number of women, they concern all those faced with this type of situation.

The initial phase, phase 1, when violence breaks out in the middle of an argument, is a shock. Especially when, as in my case, violence is not a family habit. If you've never experienced it before, it comes crashing down on you, leaving you speechless and on the brink of incomprehension. And then, as if emerging from a nightmare, the anger subsides, giving way to a calm and cheerful mood that makes you wonder if you weren't dreaming...

So we try to understand it, to justify this lapse, this unexpected outburst. We prefer to forget it. Forget about it. It won't happen again.

And when this happens again, in an insidious way, denial sets in, reinforced by the good times that follow the bad and which, at least initially, are in the majority.

What's a moment of irritation, a gesture of anger, a bad mood, compared to the enthusiastic plans for life, the tender hugs, the comforting phrases he lavishes on you in the quiet hours?

Denial lasts a long time because it protects you from the gaze of others. It sets up a glass pane between the appearance of the family or the perfect couple and the intimate truth. It's rooted in pride rather than cowardice. Pride, because we refuse to be so wrong, we don't want to accept being treated this way, no, we refuse to put up with it. Acknowledging and dealing with violence is a sign of failure, an admission of a basic lack of discernment that is difficult to accept.

Phase 2 is the shortest, because it's similar to a solution, a trial run, a little light that comes on but is suddenly extinguished. The idea, once you've accepted the violence that has begun to undermine your daily life, is to want to help the other person change, to get better. It's utopian, of course, but since there are pleasant moments, normal moments when, indeed, the perfect family is not a role for composition, we tell ourselves that it must be possible to play this role all the time. All you need to do is understand the roots of your anger, the principles of behavior, and then change should be possible.

Sometimes it's even possible to talk to the person concerned: during lulls in the action, he or she may embrace the idea. Pitfall. He has no desire to do so and will use this phase against you ("She manipulated me, she wanted me to change, she didn't accept me as I was", with a variation: "I made so much effort when she pretended to want to change me").

The pervert is in a pattern of repetition and never learns from his mistakes. Never. On the one hand, he doesn't want to, because he thinks the other person (in this case, you) is wrong, and on the other hand, he's not capable of doing so. Even the work of a shrink erodes session after session on the crest of his narcissism. Professionals today are more familiar with these patterns than they were twenty years ago, but unfortunately I'm not sure there's a real method for getting them to work on their behavior.

So, for the partner, help is a nice idea, but in practice, it's impractical and quickly abandoned. What's more, it can also irritate the temperamental person, who sees your attempts to change as a challenge to himself, which is quite unbearable for him.

Phase 3 is the longest. When all attempts at a happy, or at least serene, life have been exhausted, it's only natural that the time comes to adapt. You identify the good times and know how to make them last (a little) longer. You try out different scenarios to defuse crises, with varying degrees of success. We better understand how it works, so we (sometimes) succeed in thwarting dramas.

And then you start to survive. You're no longer trying to be happy, you're trying to stay calm. You're no longer interested in the perfect image, but in normality, justifying any deviant behavior ("He didn't come to dinner after all, he had work to do", you explain, even though in reality he left in the morning, slamming all the doors). Because life is hard enough without having to explain it to those closest to you.

We develop survival strategies, and every day that goes by without a hitch is a day gained. This phase lasts a long time, because it's exhausting and drains us of our fighting energy. All our strength is concentrated on the method to be adopted, one moment at a time. Days, weeks, months go by and we keep our heads under water, with the occasional breath to keep us going.

And then, the last phase, phase 4, can be triggered by any event. Sometimes trivial, sometimes a tidal wave.

I have a friend who left because her husband brought her (once again) a sweetened coffee, even though she'd been drinking it without sugar for twenty years: "That day, I understood that he didn't give a damn about me, my person, my tastes."

Another: "I should have taken note, as I hate green and my fiancé, at the time, gave me emeralds...."

Yet another told me that one morning her husband wanted to force her son to drink a glass of orange juice. He got so angry that he broke the glass in his mouth. She left the same evening: "It wasn't the first barbaric act, but I can't say why, that day it was the gesture too far...."

As for me, I needed the anonymous setting of a restaurant and, above all, the idea of going to the ends of the earth, under his thumb. I wouldn't have been able to do it the night before.

In phase 4, the veil is brutally torn and the loss of feelings comes into full view. This "I don't love him anymore" is something we all take a long time to admit to ourselves. And in the name of this loss of love, we finally allow ourselves to free ourselves.

There's only one solution: escape. No other alternative. Violent men are irrational and can't be reasoned with in the long term.

To get through it, you really need to distance yourself, geographically and morally. And that's difficult when there are children involved.

The justice system and its representatives always explain their decisions in the name of the child's best interests. But each case is so different. Sending children to a narcissistically perverse father condemns their equilibrium, and plunges them into suffering for which they are ill-equipped.

Today, I'm convinced that children need calm and stability more than a parent at any price. When they grow up, they will know how to ask for their father and go and see him, even if their mother is abusive and has turned them against him. A violent father, especially psychologically, is destructive. An absent father can reappear in a child's life at an age when he can defend himself.

A child once said to me:

"Why do I have to go to Dad's? He scares me...

- When you're older, you can decide if you don't want to go anymore...

- It's not fair, it's now that I'm little that I can't defend myself..."

She was 8 years old.

Justice is based on facts, and perverts know how to use facts, shaping them to their proper truth. They are ambush personalities who force social workers and psychologists to swallow their words with a vengeance.

"The children are very good with their father, they seem very calm and they all say they love their father. That said, the boy (Jean) deplores his father's abusive comments about his mother and the girls don't want to go alone (without their brother) to their father's house..."

That, in essence, was the report of the investigator who followed our family after my divorce. The judge, in the light of this brilliant analysis, concluded that I was probably lax and that my children, as a result, had difficulty with authority...

That was twenty years ago, but I can't really see any change. The 30% of fathers who have applied for custody of their children and been denied it are listened to a lot, and with great media fanfare. But when it comes to children who denounce the violent remarks of an aggressive father, the courts pay little heed. Most of the time, fathers who reclaim their children return them to the mother when they get their lives back together (or review the custody arrangement). Mothers integrate their children, whatever the changes in their lives.

Laws can't be applied to individual cases. But if today we could identify and name the perverse parent, it would already be a step forward.

Listening to other people who had gone through similar experiences made me realize that I was not alone and that it was very difficult to get out of the clutches of a pervert, and especially difficult to get out without damage.

In turn, I wanted to help other women who, like me, may feel worthless and crushed by guilt. To tell them that it is possible to get out of this hellish spiral. There are women who have succeeded, with even less means than me, who had a family, a job and faithful friends. I'm thinking of my friend Liliane, who left her four children with her husband before she was able to get them back with a job, of Lise who spent two years in a hostel with her two young children, of Marthe who spent years in hiding to escape a violent husband. Their courage and determination to escape are a source of encouragement.

Love is never suffering. A happy life cannot be woven around constant effort, permanent nervous tension and lies "to keep the peace".

A better life is always possible. You have to make choices, be prepared to give up certain material things. But freedom is too precious to be traded.

And freedom is an integral part of happiness: without freedom, there can be no happy life.

APPENDIX 1
HOW CAN WE HELP VICTIMS OF PERVERTS?

What can I do, and why tell my story, if it's of no use to others?

I'm sure that by lifting a corner of the veil on what are somewhat pejoratively referred to as "battered women", it will be easier to detect the perverts and find ways to help those who have fallen prey to them.

Whichever couple, colleague or close friend is experiencing this situation, you'll be able to detect it if you've been confronted with a pervert yourself. But for the rest of us, how can we help when we don't know what's going on, when all we see is an unhappy or unhappy friend?

Far from the cliché of the violent man, the drunken brute who beats up his wife on drunken nights and has received little or no education, it's important to understand that perverted men evolve in all walks of life. And they're hard to spot because their appearance is often that of Prince Charming. Often from a good background, well-educated, well-mannered and sometimes very principled (gallantry, civility), they can impress with their good manners. Like Janus, he has two faces, one for the exterior, which is extremely credible, and one for the intimacy he gradually reveals.

For the pervert knows that he is perverted, the violent man knows that he is violent. But he doesn't reflect on his personality, he pursues an incessant and inexorable quest that annihilates his reflection: the culmination of his pleasure, the enjoyment of his absolute desire, omnipotence over the rest of the world. The outside world is a means, a hunting ground, and then, like the cat with its prey, he plays endlessly with the coveted object, until total annihilation.

If one of your loved ones seems to you to be the victim of a pervert, avoid criticizing her partner or trying to "open her eyes". This will only strengthen her justification, as she'll feel judged. Simply be there for her, offer to take her out, show that you're available for her, and give her the impression that she's an appreciable, valuable person. The day she makes up her mind, she'll ask you for help all the more easily if you haven't been critical of her and her relationship.

Don't confine her to the role of victim either. She'll need to rebuild herself, and to do that, you have to accept her share of responsibility for her history. Women who are under the yoke of a pervert have great difficulty maintaining their self-esteem. Don't ask, as I've been asked, "Why didn't you leave earlier? Because that question is already running round and round in your head, and at first you don't know how to answer it. The right question is: "What do you want to do? Or, "How can I help you? I was lucky enough to have friends, real friends, who helped me move, find a place to live, look after my children, paint my apartment... I needed to be surrounded, not questioned.

If you come into contact with someone who lives with a pervert, don't give the impression that you're judging them. Treat her like a normal person, with a normal life. But don't hesitate to check up on them, to ask them frankly how they're doing, to surround them with your presence without being compassionate. Pitying her can already be perceived as judgmental. Avoid moralizing about willpower, divorce and its harmful effects. And don't hesitate to tell your story if your experience can help her.

No two stories are alike. But the more we talk about perverse manipulation, the more testimonies there will be on the subject, the more those who are victims will be able to recognize themselves and overcome their difficulties. It's said that experience doesn't help others, but I believe in setting an example. If I've been able to get out of it, others can too.

Appendix 2
Characteristics of the Narcissistic Pervert

The pervert is a maniac: everything has its place and a place for everything (and only he decides). If you sense that he's putting your coat away somewhere other than where you hung it when you arrived, or if he's clearing up and starting the dishes while you're having dessert, beware... The perverse person reassures himself with an order all his own, and the slightest change irritates him, just as unimportant details (you leave your handbag lying on a chair) soon become "your unbearable carelessness".

Beware: the maniac is not necessarily a neat freak. He may not vacuum, but he may power-wash his kitchen every day, pulling out all the furniture. Being a neat freak doesn't mean he'll be much help with the housework, only that you'll have to comply with his housekeeping requirements.

Perverse people have a special relationship with money. He can be stingy, since he's turned in on himself, and will only buy what he wants and what's intended for his own use. If he does offer you something, it will be something that pleases him first. If he wants to buy you a suit, it will be according to his own criteria, affirmed as being in good taste, yours being relegated to the generic term of "crappy taste".

The first few times, he'll invite you, but he'll go out of his way to point it out to you, making it clear what it cost him ("It's an expensive restaurant, did you like it?"). He can also make you feel guilty: "I wanted to please you, but it's not cheap." These kinds of little phrases are not insignificant and should set off signals in your head instead of trying to justify his words ("It's normal, he's sensitive, he wants to be sure to please me..."). No, he simply can't stop counting the money he's spent on you. Likewise, he's always checking the bill, and he's always worried about "getting ripped off" (including by you).

The pervert has a very particular way of talking. At first, you find him quick-witted, a good listener, seemingly interested in you (in reality, he's observing you to get to know your flaws). He's erudite and has a (strong) opinion on everything. You'll soon realize that conversation with him is a monologue, punctuated by interjections directed at you ("Isn't it?"; "Do you agree?"; "Do you think so?"), and you can only nod once or twice (approvingly, if possible). Any contradictory reasoning quickly turns into a confrontation, even over trifles. You can spend the whole evening trying to explain why you hate tripe. He loves them, and your lack of taste is obvious, so he won't listen to you and may even order the dish to convince you. The best thing to do is say you're allergic to it. It's unstoppable.

Because, as a corollary of the pervert, he has a great fear of illness and germs, and is quickly at a loss when faced with health concerns. Saying you've got the flu and need to take anti-biotics can help keep him away. Especially if you tell him that contagion is possible. On the other hand, if he's ill himself, you're obliged to assist him like a nurse, otherwise he could die...

In his eyes, the pervert is first and foremost a victim. When he tells you about his life, he's had bad luck, his parents bullied him, his teachers punished him for no reason, he has few or no friends (an important sign, or else he has one or two friends with whom he regularly gets angry). At work, he's misunderstood, others suck. He often has a pathological relationship with his mother, either very fusional, or hatred that he transfers to other women. Often there's an ambivalence between hate and love. Whatever happens, it's never his fault, let alone his own. He was unlucky, period. Here again, don't try to reason with him, to show him the positive aspects. You've got to play along and feel sorry for him.

The pervert is definitely unfit for happiness. He's not interested in being happy, and he's even less interested in making you happy. He thrives on conflict, and that's how he relates to you. You often see him tormented and unhappy, and he's happy with you. (Which, unfortunately, can flatter you, making you believe that you're THE one for him). Since he doesn't want to be happy, it's important to realize that you'll never be happy with someone like him. This is a good question to ask yourself at the start of a relationship: "Am I happy when I'm with him?"

Perverse people are constantly questioning themselves. You're always at fault, for everything, in every field. It's a way of constantly proving his superiority over you. There's no area of competence - children, housework, cooking, professional activity - that escapes his supremacy. He's always giving you advice, at best (and criticizing at worst). You'll never be able to do anything together. He has to do things his own way: if you're cooking, he'll be on your back, stirring, re-salting, uncovering or covering pots and pans, showering you with irritating advice; if you're helping the kids with their homework, he'll be talking at the same time as you, cutting you off, getting annoyed. Doing things with him means, at best, acting as his stooge (keeping tools close at hand, washing dishes after him), at worst acting as his outlet, and you'll be the cause of any failure (from a burnt roast to a picture frame that won't hang on the wall!).

The pervert constantly devalues (in line with the above state of mind). He constantly claims it's for your own good, to make you better, so you don't look ridiculous. It systematically demolishes everything you do and never gives you a second chance. Never try to learn anything from him. Not that he lacks pedagogy - he can be a good teacher - but he can't help criticizing your efforts and stigmatizing your mistakes. Don't ever ask him to explain anything to you - an argument is just around the corner. One of his favorite opening lines is: "What you don't understand...".

The pervert starts by verbally abusing you. He starts with hurtful remarks that may pass for jokes ("You've got hair like a poodle!"), or criticism of your friends and family, implying that it would be better not to see them anymore. If you contradict him, he gets angry and the tone can quickly escalate. Verbal aggression is obviously a first step before physical violence. But it doesn't have to be. Some remain at the verbal stage, which in no way diminishes the suffering and trauma. It's even more perverse, because this kind of violence leaves no visible traces. It's even more frightening for children, who don't understand it and receive it right in the face. A child who is told that his mother will go to prison if he doesn't obey, that his family will be destroyed, that he will only be able to live on the streets or in a shelter, his mother being deprived of resources, has no choice but to keep quiet and put up with it.

These destructive words can never be reported without being automatically minimized. But the pervert, who is usually intelligent, knows how to abuse without leaving any evidence, and he won't beat his child. How many of the paedo-psychiatrists of all kinds to whom my daughter reported "Daddy slaps" have been able to go further and understand the authoritarianism behind these words? It's complicated, I know, but once again, it's not enough just to ask questions, you also have to listen to the children, which, in my opinion, we still don't do enough of today.

The pervert uses blackmail and leaves you no choice. If you don't do what he wants, he'll take the children away, cut you off, break your things, drive off in the car and leave you alone in the middle of nowhere, cancel dinners, vacations, outings... When you're in the middle of the conflict and these threats are raining down on your head, accompanied by screaming and blows, you want only one thing: peace. For the argument to stop before it turns ugly, even uglier, because just when you think you've reached the bottom of the horror, the mid-point of the unjustified anger, a wave shoots up again and takes your breath away. Sometimes I understand those suspects, wrongly accused, who end up confessing anything under pressure. When you've hit rock bottom, when the insults are raining down, when your terrified children are lurking in the bedroom, you prefer to crawl on your knees and apologize, beg forgiveness, confess wrongdoing, calm things down and get on with life. There have been times when I've thrown myself into the arms of my tormentor, telling him he was right, that it was all my fault, just to ease the conflict.

Reason for what? What fault? I couldn't remember, but at the time, that wasn't the problem. The problem was to stop the outpouring of screams and the inevitable escalation of violence by any means necessary.

The pervert turns you upside down and you end up thinking he's right. You lose your temper, your children suffer and you tell yourself it's your fault.

He's often a master of rhetoric: he has arguments, he knows how to counter you, and sometimes these arguments are so huge that there's nothing left to say. You keep quiet, he thinks he's won, you nod, and he calms down. You're at the bottom of the bucket.

Any relationship that doesn't bring happiness is toxic. If you're constantly thinking that things should work out, if you try to calm him down more often than to kiss him, if when he's with you the air in the room becomes thin and the atmosphere is tinged with apprehension, then the signs are there. You've come face to face with a pervert, so don't kid yourself that the worst is yet to come.

You have to know how to ask for help and admit that you don't want to be unhappy anymore.

The magic phrase, the question to ask yourself, is not "Could I live with him", but rather "Could I live without him"? When the answer is "Yes, and even better", don't hesitate.

APPENDIX 3
WOMEN'S WORDS

The following excerpts were taken from discussion groups I attended, which helped me a great deal. Attending these kinds of meetings is a real springboard to awareness. Firstly, because it's the first step towards asking for help.

As for me, I joined a little late, thinking I could help others through my own experience. However, all these exchanges have helped to restore my equilibrium, and I have received more than I gave. I understood many of my reservations, I learned to have compassion for myself and, in the end, these groups were a real therapy. Listening to these women who reminded me of my own experiences, I was finally able to put my feelings into words, and the explanation was staring me in the face.

Of course, we always see other people's situations more clearly...

I'm not that unhappy," confided one young woman, "my husband doesn't drink, he doesn't even hit me, it's just that when

I'm with him, I always feel like I'm good for nothing, he refuses to let me work, he says it's because he loves me too much...".

He loves me so much," said a second, "that he can't do without me. I can't do anything, as soon as he's home I have to listen to him, be by his side; it's simple, if I don't watch TV with him, he gets sick of it and makes a scene... In the beginning I used to read or knit while he watched his shows, today, even that's no longer possible, he can't stand it anymore..."

"I always manage to get home before he does. If I mention it beforehand, there's a scene, and he claims that I'm too often messing around with my family, that they're turning me against him. It's not true, I never talk to them about our problems as a couple... When, at the end of his arguments, he lets me go, he tells me he's going to worry all day, because I'll be on the road (it's ten kilometers away!). So I prefer not to tell him...".

Another woman explained, convinced of the validity of her attitude:

"He doesn't like me to dress in anything other than a dress, so I wear the clothes he chooses for me...".

She was in the adaptation phase and her whole life was focused on avoiding crises... She came to the group for three years before daring to take action and leave her husband. We sensed that she was looking to others for reassurance. At first she said: "It's normal to try not to displease him, isn't it?

No. It just didn't make sense that the slightest piece of clothing would trigger a drama. And concessions like that, not too bad one by one, are multiplied tenfold in just one day. And it's unbearable. All the while, this woman was giving us examples that she considered acceptable as excuses for her husband's behavior: "It's true, you just can't get on his nerves, he tells me every day: 'If you loved me, you'd want to please me, you KNOW I don't like the closet door open and you leave it open, don't tell me you're not doing it on purpose!"

And how many women calmly explain: "No, no, there's no violence, at least much less... Of course, he still locks them in the closet or breaks their toys, but he doesn't beat them anymore...". And the psychologist who took part in our sessions, round-eyed, retorted: "Because for you that's not violence?"

It's in the eyes of others that the word violence takes on its full meaning. Even in front of other victims. Hence the important role of the group. All the stories are different, but at the same time they all resonate with each other. As I listened to each person's story, at first I thought: "No, it's not the same for me. But then a word, a phrase, a situation and the words spoken threw images of my own life back in my face.

But when for years you've heard: "It's just a jostle, oh dear! I didn't even raise my hand to him or her, I barely touched him or her..." Obviously, we no longer know what is tolerable. And neither do the children, who get used to this perverse modus operandi and never report it. This authoritarianism becomes so familiar to them that it seems normal.

Hence the importance, when a father is violent, of denouncing his behavior as unacceptable. Not to let children get used to his gestures, his cries.

A social worker once came to explain to the group how she tried to decipher the violence behind the children's words: "A child lives what he lives as the norm, so I avoid generic words, I try to dig a little, but the younger the children are the less they know how to tell... And some parents give the change perfectly..."

A friend who spent almost thirty years with an alcoholic and violent husband explained: "I knew that if I divorced him, he would have rights, including the right to have sole custody of our daughter at weekends. As long as she was little, I preferred to stay and put up with it. At least when he was drunk, I didn't let him wake her up, I channeled him. Even if I took some knocks, I couldn't have lived with the idea that she was alone and at his mercy..."

She wasted precious years, and of course we understand her reaction; but her daughter didn't have a very happy childhood. She knew that justice would be slow, that the father had rights and that her daughter could face violence, so she preferred to put herself in brackets.

Some are fighting. But the more legal action, appeals and interim injunctions we take to try and curb the pervert's actions towards the children, the longer it's going to last. I once knew a woman who fought for ten years to prevent her ex-husband from seeing their daughter alone. She suspected touching, but couldn't really prove it. After all these years, she was still at the same point and still fighting with her ex through lawyers.

Others were quicker to let go, to get some peace. This is not cowardice. It's just recognizing that fighting feeds an unhealthy bond and prevents closure.

As for the pension, the amount depends on who is considering it.

A lawyer once said ironically to a woman who was fighting for unpaid alimony: "You've got time to waste to get two hundred francs back..."

Some time later, the same lawyer calmly explained: "Finally, two hundred francs per child, that's a lot for my client! What's left for him?"

This notion of "rest" remains a real issue.

It's generally accepted that the father should have enough "left over" to live on. Which seems logical. But who cares about "leftovers" when it comes to mothers? Mothers who earn so little that everything goes to pay the bills and take care of the children? Mothers who not only don't have a "leftover", but don't even have the bare necessities?

In the words of a famous sociologist, Évelyne Sullerot, "men look after their children when they can, and mothers when they have to".

Acknowledgements

My thanks go first of all to those who supported me when I needed it, my family, my brother J.-P. (Jean-Pierre), my sister Aude, and also those who were close to me at the time, Véronique, Anne-Christine, Marie-Pierre, Sylvie, Édith, Tanya, Marthe, Serge, Pascal and Patrick...

To those who believed in this book and encouraged me, Catherine Meyer, Jean-Baptiste Bourrat and Christophe André.

To the entire Max Milo team for their patience, attentiveness and quality of work.

And of course, to Bernard, the man who lit up my life and gave me back my self-confidence.

Best sellers Max Milo Editions

Hitler's banker, Jean-François Bouchard

Confessions of a forger, Éric Piedoie Le Tiec

The Koran and the flesh, Ludovic-Mohamed Zahed

Governing by fake news, Jacques Baud

Governing by chaos, Collectif

A political history of food, Paul Ariès

Mad in U.S.A.: The ravages of the "American model",
Michel Desmurget

Mondial soccer club geopolitics, Kévin Veyssière

Putin: Game master?, Jacques Braud

Treatise on the three impostors: Moses, Jesus, Muhammad,
The Spirit of Spinoza

TV Lobotomy, Michel Desmurget

www.ingramcontent.com/pod-product-compliance
Lightning Source LLC
LaVergne TN
LVHW021606060726
842527LV00015B/3921